Escaping The Venus Trap

For The Woman Who Says, "I Don't Want It All, But I Want More Than This"

Robin Bowman

BookPartners, Inc.
Wilsonville, Oregon

BookPartners, Inc.
P.O. Box 922
Wilsonville, Oregon 97070

Dedication

Dedicated to my precious family, Lea Bowman, Luke Bowman and Peter Bowman. You set the standard for encouragement, cooperation and commitment that will enable all of humanity to escape the Venus trap.

Table Of Contents

Acknowledgements

~ ~

The biggest joy in writing this book has been the support and encouragement from the wonderful folks who gladly shared their time, talents, encouragement and stories with me.

Thorn and Ursula Bacon are wonderful publishers, editors and advisors. Without their help this book literally would still be in my word processor.

To the women who shared their stories with me to help other women like us, many thanks are due: Janet Oglethorpe, Chris Clarke-Epstein, Jane Tait, Glenda Graves, Deborah Hawker, Jill Griffin, Gail Raben, Karen Sheridan, Sandy Hogan, Barb Schwarz, Linda Coffey, Catherine Fyock, Mary Moore, Ann Humphries, Irene Levitt.

To the talented women and men who reviewed the manuscript and gave me great insights and tips, I owe a tremendous debt: Betty Bartlett, Marcia McKinley, Amy

Perkins, Kristy Davis, Larry Hampton and Peter Bowman. Audrey Salgado examined the manuscript with exquisite precision. Her wonderfully astute recommendations created excellent improvements. A special thanks to Ginger Purdy whose tireless efforts in creating a political presence for women have helped many women escape the Venus trap.

Three special women in my life I want to thank for their encouragement to pursue my dreams. Helen Coleman taught me high school biology and treasured me so that she gave me the gift of appreciating myself. Linda Hoy shared the joy of theatre and encourage me as a budding actress. Gay Norris's encouragement and brilliant insights have often helped me find my way when I was baffled about how to proceed.

Thanks to Kay Baker, my advisor in the speaking profession, who has shared encouragement and great stories. Thanks to Dick Harder and NSA - Heart of Texas, our local chapter of the National Speakers Association, for keeping me inspired and motivated. Thanks to George McKenzie for helping me get the word out about this book. And a huge round of applause for Dannet Bock who keeps my office sane and running like clockwork.

Thanks to my daughter, Lea Bowman, who we will see on the silver screen and on the stage in not so many years. Thanks to my son, Luke Bowman, who loves music and will gift the world with his beautiful music wherever his dreams lead him. May you both always pursue your dreams with your characteristic energy. Know that your mother believes you are the two neatest people on the face of the earth.

Thanks to my husband and helpmate, Peter Bowman, whose support and enthusiasm for my pursuits lead many to believe he is my personal PR agency. Thanks for believing

~ ~

in me and for your wonderfully intelligent and insightful thoughts. You are the rain that keeps me growing and escaping the Venus trap.

Robin Bowman
February 28, 1996

Introduction

~ ~

"It is never too late to be what you might have been."

George Elliot

When I was five, I crashed into the Venus Trap. I was the second oldest of five children, three girls and two boys. My father took charge of getting us dressed every Sunday morning. Not wanting our Sunday clothes to get dirty, he would bark, "Put on your shorts, t-shirts, shoes and socks." He meant for the boys to put on their shorts and t-shirts, but for the girls to put on their slips and panties. This went on for months and months.

I felt left out. I wanted to be noticed. One day, a creative idea popped into my head. "Here's how I can let Daddy know how I feel!" Tickled with myself at the witty way I would enlighten my dad, I could hardly wait for Sunday to come. I was sure the joke would delight my dad, as well as convince him to include the girls in his command.

The next Sunday I found a pair of my shorts from the summer before. I rummaged in my brothers' dresser drawers and got a t-shirt. I put on the shorts and t-shirt, and my shoes and socks. Feeling like an actress on opening night, I went down to breakfast. Much to my surprise, my father missed the cleverness and inventiveness of my joke. He took it as insubordination. I was punished with a belting.

Unwittingly, I tumbled into the Venus trap. I detected that our society devalues the female perspective and discourages female achievement. Since then, I have personally experienced and seen other women experience many other examples of the Venus trap. Time and again I see talented, capable women undermined by the Venus trap. I am appalled by the waste of human talent. Perhaps you have noticed it too.

Like me, maybe you have tried to fit the role of "woman" rather than the role of "human." You may have been caught in the Venus trap — struggling with feminine stereotypes, the Venus image, and a society that gives you permission to pursue professional endeavors, as long as your housework is done first. Even when you have managed to maintain both the career and the family, you are bombarded with news reports asking, "Is day care good for the children?" You want the best for your family and your relationships, and you end up exhausted.

You constantly hear, "Can women have it all?" You don't want it all. You are happy to give up laundry, toilets, and cooking supper. Small wonder that research shows 59% of women and 65% of men think it is easier to be a man than a woman. No one questions that a man will pursue his dreams and have a wife and family.

~ ~

Where are the systems to support you? Is there no way out of this bind?

You may have found yourself asking these questions:

What do I want to be when I grow up?

Why is balancing family and career so tough?

Why does everyone else seem so confident?

Why do I feel so empty and unfulfilled?

How can I create a life I love without leaving those I love?

If you're like me, you have found yourself saying, "There's got to be more than this." Many of us have tried pursuing the prevailing model of success and have become tired and frustrated.

I've discovered that there is a way out. You can create your own definition of success. You can escape the Venus trap. You can realize your innate potential and arrange your life to please yourself. You can find balance in your life while pursuing your dreams. Many women have made it work.

I believe we need a new strategy for women that considers the challenges that only women face. We need a female strategy that acknowledges us for ourselves while acknowledging the challenges that limit our dreams. We need to escape the Venus trap, rather than be encouraged to follow its false illusion.

Having a life strategy is foreign to many of us. I'll bet you did not consider your profession, much less your life, carefully. I'll bet your family and friends assumed that you would be supported by a husband and that your professional life was secondary. But the statistics show that you cannot count on one husband to support you throughout your life. Frequently, the wife has played a supportive role throughout the husband's career development phase of life, only to find

~ ~

herself divorced, unemployed and unprepared for the work world after she has helped her spouse establish himself professionally. Most women can look forward to many years of single life in which their livelihood will be dependent on their own earning power.

Even if you've developed an independent career, often you have depended on a single job to provide your sole source of financial support. In the present economic climate of downsizing, you cannot depend on keeping the job you have forever. Therefore, it is in your best interest to develop a life strategy that includes multiple options of earning a living.

In 1988, I began my consulting and speaking business. I began helping businesses develop strategic plans. Because all businesses have limited resources, to succeed in the marketplace they must take a strategic approach. My work with companies led me to develop a five-step process for strategic planning. Using this five-step process, companies maximize their results. This five-step process begins with the big picture — the dream, and proceeds to break the dream down into successively smaller chunks. The five steps are:

- Dream
- Discovery
- Development
- Design
- Diligence

As I began to work with women to help them increase their success, I realized that this approach could be applied to the challenges that we, as women, face in our lives. You have limited resources (time, energy, money.) But if you apply the same strategic process to your life, the results are amazing.

To escape the Venus trap, to take charge of your life, to define it on your own terms, you must take a strategic approach. Taking a strategic approach to your life gives you control, flexibility and power. You would never begin to bake a cake without a recipe, nor build a home without a blueprint. Yet I'll bet you spend more time planning your two-week vacation than you do planning the two thousand or more hours per year that you spend working. Isn't that ridiculous?

American author and essayist, Dorothy Canfield Fisher, underscored the importance of a life strategy when she observed:

"If we would only give, just once, the same amount of reflection to what we want to get out of life that we give to the question of what to do with a two-week vacation, we would be startled at our false standards and the aimless procession of our busy days."

The five-step process I've developed allows you to adapt it for your life. By taking a strategic approach that recognizes the realities of a female life, you can begin to maximize pleasure from both your work life and your personal life. The two are inextricably connected. The five-step process recognizes this vital connection and shows you how to positively change both aspects to increase your fulfillment.

Dream: Your personal dreams lay the foundation for a fulfilling life, so the first of the five steps explores the question: "Where do I want to be?" Since you spend the bulk of your life earning a living, to achieve satisfaction you must align your life work with your natural interests, preferences and strengths. By exploring your dreams, you'll find surprising methods to balance your achievement

~ ~

desires with your relationship desires.

Discovery: The second of the five steps, discovery, explores and answers the question: "Where am I now?" It prompts you to discover what raw materials you have to work with, your limitations, and your opportunities. Within this step, you explore the strengths and resources you have and investigate the considerations you must balance to advance your dreams. You uncover patterns and assumptions that may have led you into the Venus trap.

Design: "How do I get to where I want to be?" is addressed by the third, or design step. What goals and objectives must you design to achieve your dream? The design step is the road map phase of the overall strategy. To move toward your desired dream, you must take the steps necessary to create your dream.

Development: Step four, the development step, answers the question: "What methods do I use?" What you need to know and where you go to get it is addressed in this phase. You begin to acquire the know-how and to build the foundations to lead you on your path.

Diligence: The diligence step is the fifth phase of your development plan, and it answers the question: "How do I stay where I've arrived and what do I do next?" You measure your progress and you begin the cycle again.

When you have explored the five steps, your life will begin to take the shape you want it to express.

Through living your dreams you not only improve your own life, you improve the world for all people. You can help create a society that empowers women as human beings with normal human desires for achievement and self-expression. You escape the Venus trap.

Chapter One
Dream

~ ~

Reach high, for stars lie hidden in your soul.
Dream deep, for every dream precedes the goal.
— *Pamela Vaull Starr*

What would you be doing right this minute if you could be doing anything in the world? Take a minute to enjoy that thought. Wouldn't it be nice if you could actually make that thought a reality in your life? You can!

"Whoa, wait a minute there," you say. "Now you've gone off the deep end and we're barely into the book! I can't possibly do that."

The fact is you practice a form of self-deception frequently. One example is at the movies when you suspend your disbelief for a while and agree to believe what is happening on the screen. All of us know that the heroine doesn't really win the marathon race. But we cheer her on just the same. Movie makers call our voluntary deception

~ ~

the "willing suspension of disbelief." Without the willing suspension of disbelief, movies wouldn't be any fun. We would watch and continually say to ourselves: "No way. They never could have done that."

To benefit from the dream step in reinventing your life, you have to adopt a similar "willing suspension of disbelief." Suspend judgement on the practicality of your dream until later. Right now the idea is for you to dream. Later on, you will address how to make your dream a reality. You can't do that step until you know what your dream is. Look into your past to discover your dream. So, I ask you again what would you be doing right this minute if you could be doing anything in the world?

Perhaps as a child you dreamed of an exciting future like Mae Jemison did. Born in 1956, Mae Jemison dreamed of being an astronaut. As a child growing up on the south side of Chicago, she was often "looking up at the stars, wondering what was up there, knowing I'd go up there someday, though I didn't know how." When she saw the Gemini and Apollo space flights on TV, she knew she would one day be aboard. "Very clearly, I was sure I wanted to go into space even if there had never been any astronauts."[1]

Jemison found that people discouraged her dream to become the first black female astronaut. Even her kindergarten teacher told her that her dream of being a physician first, and astronaut next was too lofty. "Don't you mean you want to be a nurse?"

Undaunted, Jemison became a physician, and then applied to the NASA program. Even after becoming an astronaut, some people reacted with disbelief. "Some people say I don't look like an astronaut. But that's okay ... because I am ... all peoples of the world have astronomers, physicists, and explorers."[2]

Jemison doesn't consider herself to be a role model, although she obviously is a great example of pursuing your dream. She recognizes, however, that each person's dream may be different. "The thing that I've done throughout my life is to do the best job that I can and to be me. And that's really all I can do. In terms of being a role model ... what I'd like to be is someone who said, 'No, don't try to necessarily be like me or live your life or grow up to be an astronaut or a physician — unless that's what you want to do.' I believe you should do things you want to do, regardless of whether anyone's been there before."[3]

It doesn't make any difference whether or not your dream is similar to Mae Jemison's or is quite different. To escape the Venus trap, you need to align your life with your dream, whatever it is. The importance of this alignment cannot be overemphasized. You may have knocked yourself out to accomplish one-dimensional goals which, when achieved, seem unworthy of the effort. The *Wall Street Journal* commented on this common disappointment: "'When driven people reach a goal, they don't enjoy it,' explains New York psychiatrist Jeffrey Kahn. 'They feel let down and quickly pick up another project. When something unexpected comes up, they can't adapt.'"[4]

As a human being you naturally want to contribute to the world around you. You also want to stretch your wings and fly in the direction that appeals to you. You see many ways to improve the world and you know things are happening that you don't like. Perhaps your dream reflects making those changes. But if you're like most people I've met, you may not have stopped to define your purpose exactly.

As women, we have not been trained or encouraged to think of dreams for ourselves. In the traditional "helping" roles and jobs, we have assisted others to achieve their dreams, but we have fallen far short of visualizing our own.

Dreaming about material things is not the kind of dream I mean. The dream of possessing some material item — a car, a house, a stereo system — frequently is a cover-up for a need that is not being met elsewhere. Material acquisitions are often the consolation prizes: if I can't have my dream, I will settle for a car.

Worthwhile dreams are not about acquisitions. They about who you are, not about what you have. Worthwhile dreams lead you to know how you wish to express your essence. Worthwhile dreams are about using your talents, flexing your human abilities, figuring out what your purpose is on earth. Dreams are about lifting your tired vision from the day-to-day demands and looking at who you really are. What contribution to the world would you be making if you aligned your life with your essence?

By determining your dream, you tap into your creativity and the power of what you care passionately about.

Whose Dream Are You Living?

> Dreams are necessary to life.
> — *Anaïs Nin*

I'll bet the messages you got when you were growing up were similar to mine, certainly not designed to help me express my dream nor to discover who I was. Here's what I heard: "Girls should get educated so that they can get a job if their husband dies." I was also told I should become a teacher so that I would be home when the kids got out of school. Choosing a profession based on the assumption that you will marry, that your husband will be the primary breadwinner, and therefore you only need a backup source of income, is a darn poor way to decide the direction of your life.

Well, of course, I listened to the voices of advice, married at age 20 and got my teaching degree. After three years of teaching, I found myself sitting behind my desk with my chin on my hands complaining and wondering to myself, "I'm going to be doing this for *forty* more years?"

I was completely miserable. Don't get me wrong. Teaching is perhaps the noblest profession of all, and certainly not for the faint-hearted. I completely agree with Ann Richards. After teaching government and history at a junior high school in Austin for a year, she came to the conclusion: "Teaching was the hardest work I had ever done, and it remains the hardest work I have done to date."[5] The problem was that teaching was not a good match for me personally. Unfortunately, after 26 years of forgetting about my dream, it took me a long time to remember it and put it into action.

Getting to Know Yourself

"... It isn't until you come to a spiritual understanding of who you are — not necessarily a religious feeling, but deep down, the spirit within — that you can begin to take control."

— *Oprah Winfrey*

Getting to know yourself is crucial to finding your dream. To get to know yourself, try spending a day in silence. A day spent in silence is a remarkable beginning to dream discovery. If you can, go to a place which is special to you, maybe in the country or at the seashore. Get a buddy to go along with you if you want company, but agree with her to be silent for the entire day. Some amazing discoveries are in store for you.

I was first exposed to a day of silence at a workshop I attended. When I heard we were going to spend a day without conversation, I felt ripped off.

"I spent all this money on this workshop to get information and we're going to keep our mouths shut for a whole day?" My attitude was quite different by the time the day of silence ended. That period of quiet was one of the greatest gifts I have ever experienced. It gave me my lifetime dream to become a professional speaker. I learned that only in silence can we delve inside ourselves for the valuable things we have previously been distracted from.

Once you've taken the plunge into the calmness inside you, ask yourself, "What would I be doing if I could do anything in the world?" Be truly honest with yourself and banish the doubting little voice that says, "Yeah, but where would I get the money?" or "Yeah, but my mother would disown me." If you need an answer for the voice of doubt, ask yourself what if you had all the money in the world and your mother wanted you to be true to yourself? What would you do then? In your answer to that question lies the beginning of your dream.

In your precious day of silence, listen carefully to your dream. Then put your dream on paper. Write it out. You will be surprised by the results when you write your intentions down.

Do not judge your answers as you go. Remember the idea of willing suspension of disbelief? That's what you must do to drown out the internal critic that says: "Who do you think you are?" Or, "That will never work." Convince your critic that you're doing this for fun and no one will witness the process. Then, keep your pen moving. Write whatever pops into your mind as you answer the following questions:

1. What would I be doing if I could do anything in the world?
2. What was I doing at age nine?
3. What would I like to accomplish if time and money were no object?
4. What do I want to accomplish with the rest of my life?
5. What do I love to do?
6. What three successes have I had that I am proud of and why?
7. What do I want people to say about me when I am dead?
8. What would I like to be doing in five years?
9. What is my dream? Write out your dream for the next five years.
10. What small step can I take to put more of my dream into my life today?

Who is that Mysterious Person in the Mirror?

If between the dirty diapers and the run in your pantyhose, you have forgotten what you love, don't feel all alone. For many of us women, ignoring our dream is a gender-related hazard.

One major clue to your intended dream is to look at what you love. Native American writer Jose Hobday's father used to say, "Try many things. When you find what you love, do that. Then figure out how to make a living with

~ ~

it." Hobday concludes: "Breaking society up into duty and earning, having and wanting — that can be bondage."[6]

What do you feel impassioned about? What moves you, makes your interest quicken, raises your sense of yourself? When you discover what you love best and choose your life's work based on what you love, you tap into the power of that passion and you find success flowing from that power. It's unstoppable! You must do what you love in order to create success.

It doesn't matter what the nature of your dream is. You may want to arrange flowers, read to mountain kids in Appalachia, or be the first woman president of IBM. Only one person has to understand your dream. That person is you.

Another way to discover your dream is to rediscover what you loved when you were age nine. What types of things did you do as you played? What types of play did you love? At nine, girls have not yet succumbed to putting themselves last. By examining your childhood play, you can rediscover what you loved best.

When I was nine, my family moved from Washington, D.C. to Ft. Sill, Oklahoma. My father was in the Army and we were to live on the Army post. When we arrived, we had to wait for our quarters to become ready and so we spent several days living in the guest quarters. In the park behind the guest quarters was an amphitheater with a large stage area. The park was deserted and I spent some of the happiest hours of my life pretending to be a great actress on that stage. Later on in school, my best friend, Rachel, and I adapted fairy tales into plays, and staged them. We did everything from creating sets to making costumes to playing the leading roles.

By the time I was choosing a career, I had forgotten all

~ ~

about how I loved to create and to present. Only later when I wondered why my career choices had left me so dry did I discover that I needed to include creating and presenting. Out of that discovery I developed my business as a professional speaker and writer.

Your passions may be quite different. You may have loved Barbies, catching fireflies or playing Indians in the woods. Whatever it is that you loved to do, recapture it and try to incorporate some part of it into your present life. Ask yourself: "What was it about catching fireflies that I loved?" Maybe it was running freely out-of-doors. Maybe it was the feeling of success that exhilarated you as you achieved your goals. By identifying what you loved about what you did, you will discover clues to what you love now and you can add present day activities that match it.

What Are You Good At?

"Oh," many women say, "I'm not good at much of anything." Not true. Each one of us is good at something. We may not notice those activities that give us intense pleasure and that we do well. I agree with Jim Cathcart, a nationally known speaker. He says the question is not "How talented are you?" but rather, "What are your talents?"

Try writing out three successes you have had. Go ahead. No one is looking. Don't get caught up worrying about spelling or grammar. No one will see this but you. Describe those successes and the feelings you've had in great detail. What did you do to create them? What is it that those three achievements had in common? Would you like more of that kind of success in the future? How can you set up your work so that you can recreate the pleasure you derived from those accomplishments?

~ ~

Besides looking internally to know yourself better, looking at other women gives you clues as well. The next chapter explores successful women.

Let Your Dream Grow

"I've dreamt in my life dreams that have stayed with me ever after, and changed my ideas; they've gone through and through me, like wine through water, and altered the color of my mind."

— *Emily Brontë*

Your dream is not something you discover once and never question again. It is more like a rosebud opening. At first, it looks one way and later it opens more fully and you understand it in a different way. Don't stop your whole life while you wait for your dream to unfold.

Try different things. How do they feel to you? Yes? No? Go on to the next thing you think you might like to try. It is in the trying that you discover what your dream really is. A dream is discovered and flowers as you live. Perhaps your dream must be rediscovered because once you knew it but now have forgotten it. Dreams are important because they bring you back to your own internal map and project it into the future. What do you want to be and become?

Never have the opportunities been greater than they are in the world today. The challenge to us as women is to stretch beyond our previous society-imposed limitations (which later became self-imposed limitations). It takes courage to dream and overcome the limitations we have absorbed from our environment. Then, it takes even more courage to take action to make the dream happen.

Don't worry about whether the dream you determine

now is your "true" one. Often, the masterpiece of your true self has been painted over by so many layers of false assumptions that it takes many repetitions until you can finally uncover the original you. To get to the masterpiece, you must begin peeling back the coatings of camouflage hiding the real you. My professional career has been a series of layer removals. Every layer I uncovered helped me understand my dream. My first two positions were secretarial. My third was as a teacher. I discovered from these what I didn't want to do. Then, I started a manufacturing business. Although it was a tremendous learning experience, I knew this was not what I wanted to pursue either. After a chance encounter with a manager who needed a writer for technical documentation, I began a technical writing business.

At first, I didn't know much about the field and the learning was tremendously fun for me. I loved the challenge. Soon, however, it became easy. Then, the job became routine. I sat in front of a computer screen inserting style commands into a document. Although I was being paid what I thought were unbelievably high rates, I was bored and longed for a new challenge.

I returned to school, earned my M.B.A., and then started consulting to small businesses. Finding small businesses unprofitable, I decided to evolve into speaking and consulting. I found my niche. I love the speaking, writing and consulting. As I sit on my deck overlooking a beautiful green field clicking away on my laptop, I realize I am living my dream life! Even so, I know I will uncover more layers as I continue to grow.

Now in the tenth year of her speaking business, Barb Schwarz, discovered that her dream changed along the way. Barb started her business in her basement. At first, she

~ ~

dreamed of building a big company, and her company grew to 21 employees. She rented a big retail space. However, she found she was spending 45-50 weeks a year on the road to cover the huge overhead and provide for her employees. "You think that bigger is better. It isn't always," says Barb. She decided to downsize her company, and go to suppliers to provide services such as telemarketing, promotions and sponsors. Now, her company has four and one half employees including Barb and her husband. Last year, she spent 38 weeks on the road. Her goal is to reduce that to 30. Her business has expanded from real estate into the personal growth market, offering inspirational programs on spirit, mind, and body. Although she has considered working with other markets, Barb feels she is exactly where she is supposed to be. "My life is a great gift and a great honoring, a great blessing. It's a miracle," says Barb.

When I asked Sandy Hogan of Portland, Oregon, "When did you first know what you wanted to do in your life?" she said, "I'm not sure I know that yet. I am a work in progress." Each step in Sandy's life led her from one dream to another; one layer closer to her masterpiece.

The role models she saw for women were moms, nurses or teachers. The women she wanted to emulate were English teachers, so she first resolved to be a teacher. After graduating from college with a degree in English and Drama, she decided she needed an adventure. When she was in college, she had once looked up, seen a jet fly by, and said, "I want to do that." So she became a cabin attendant for Pan Am and flew around the world. After flying for a year, she was laid off from Pan Am. Having had enough of being a cabin attendant, she decided to pursue her teaching career.

She first taught in a very small town in California, then

decided she wanted to move to a larger town and did. While she was teaching, she met her husband, a police officer.

When California rolled back the tax base making the future look bleak for both teachers and police officers, Sandy went to Washington State to investigate possibilities. "Come up," she told her family. "We're moving."

Though Sandy had concluded that Washington was a much better location for them, she didn't find any teaching positions. She accepted a job at Safeco Life Insurance in Seattle to become a marketing coordinator. Finding that she didn't like the strict behavior expected of her there, she moved to the Federal Home Loan Bank. In that position, she traveled over eight western states. She says, "The west was worth winning."

In 1982, Sandy took a job as marketing coordinator for a software company marketing a program to help teachers with grading and scheduling. So green in technology that she spelled software "softwear," Sandy nevertheless thrived in the company and by 1986, she was asked to speak on a panel for the Washington Software Association on "Marketing Practices for Emerging Companies." Also on the panel were employees from Microsoft and Aldus. The representative from Aldus told Sandy, "You seem well-connected in the industry." Aldus was building management staff at the time, and the man told her that his company was looking for a few good people. He told Sandy he was looking at her for a senior marketing position. Sandy wasn't interested in changing companies, but Aldus was persuasive, and Sandy loved the feel of the new company. The offer also included lucrative stock options.

By 1992, the stock options had paid off, but Sandy had paid even more dearly in terms of health and family. "I was rode hard and put up wet," Sandy said in imitation western slang. "I did twelve years work in six years, but I learned great lessons in the trenches." She loved the exhilarating work with her bright colleagues, but Sandy decided that it was time to move on. "Everything has a price and I was no longer willing to pay that price."

Beginning her own firm, she pursued consulting and writing for a year and a half, but missing the software industry connection, accepted a top post with the Software Association of Oregon. She learned a great lesson from this experience. She says, "Be clear about what you want. Be aware the universe will deliver it to you in a way you cannot imagine."

Now, Sandy is active in the local theater and the Friends of the Library. She takes art classes and singing lessons. Though the family income is not what it used to be, she and her husband are more open to the joy of life. "You can't fill an empty belly with money. You must fill it with joy." Now, she says, she is run by desire. She constantly asks herself: "What do I want to do?" In looking back over her life, she thinks: "Isn't this a great life?" Each layer led Sandy closer and closer to her dream. Now, she is living her dream life, and she may yet discover another layer.

Chapter Two
Study Successful Women

~ ~

"I believe there is something unexplored about
woman that only a woman can explore."
— *Georgia O'Keefe*

By looking at women who have managed to arrange
their lives in ways that are pleasing to them despite society's
expectations, we can often gain great insights into how we
can live our own lives more true to our dreams. We do not
necessarily want to emulate every successful woman we
study. But by recognizing what they have done and our
response to it, we can learn a great deal about ourselves.

As you study the women described in this chapter, ask
yourself these questions:

"Are these the dreams I would have if I dared?"

"Do I identify with this particular woman?"

"Do I find this woman inspiring, or do I dislike the way
she lived her life?"

~ ~

"How did she overcome the obstacles that I face?"

Often speakers and authors say to me, "I would like to include more examples of women, but it is hard to find them." While it is true that more men have been written about than women, there are many books with information on successful women. (Ones I have found enjoyable are listed in the reference section at the back of this book.) Studying successful men may be instructional. Keep in mind, however, that every successful woman had to overcome the same performance obstacles encountered by the men. In addition, every successful woman has overcome the social and cultural gender roadblocks that only women face. By finding out how outstanding women achieved their successes, we can learn methods to achieve our own goals. Following are a few inspirational women: first from historical times; then from modern times.

Successful Women from History

Women were successful even back in the golden days of Greece. Aspasia was the teacher of Plato and Socrates. She later became the wife of Pericles, ruler of Athens, and wrote the speeches that brought him fame. (Behind every successful Greek man was a woman, also!) Pericles was too strong to criticize, so Athenians attacked Aspasia. She became, in the words of one twentieth-century historian, "One of the first women to be forced to run through the whole gamut of scorn, satire, and abuse because of her independence, her self-reliance, and her freedom from ordinary prejudice."[7]

When prejudice prevented women from entering certain professions, they used creative means to pursue their dreams. To do as they chose, many women disguised themselves as men. Dr. James Barry disguised herself as a man and began her medical studies in 1810 in Edinburgh. Even at the time of her death in 1865, women were not allowed to attend medical school in England. She served for 46 years as a top British Army medical officer. She was considered an excellent doctor, and her gender was discovered only when she died.[8]

It is estimated 400 women disguised themselves as men to pose as soldiers during the Civil War. Sarah Emma Edmonds was one of those 400. Historians guess she enjoyed the freedom that dressing as a male gave her. Spending most of her military career behind front lines, Edmonds was well thought of by her commanders, and she was appointed as an aide to a colonel, and was the brigade's mail carrier. As the mail carrier, she braved flooding rivers to bring letters to her unit.

Even when women began to enter fields previously closed to them, they continued to be required to adjust their pursuits because of prejudice. You may have heard of the Apgar score which all hospitals use today to identify newborn babies that are at risk. You may not know that a pioneering woman doctor, Virginia Apgar, developed the score. In spite of Apgar's talent, she gave up her dream to become a surgeon because in the 1930s she thought, "Even women won't go to a woman surgeon."[9] Instead, she trained as a physician and used her talents as an anesthesiologist and director of birth defects research.

Women are responsible for many other advancements which have benefited us. It was Elizabeth Cochrane, alias Nellie Bly, who conceived of investigative reporting, a journalistic practice that has helped prevent many abuses from occurring in our society. Bly first came to notice when she wrote an angry and articulate response to a Pittsburgh

Dispatch editorial that opposed women's suffrage and the idea of careers for women. Once, Bly had herself committed to a New York insane asylum for a week and later wrote an exposé. She got herself hired in factories and wrote about the deplorable conditions. Her journalism led to major reforms.[10]

Women have been politically astute and active in the life of our country from the beginning. While John Adams was attending the Continental Congress and contributing to the writing of the Declaration of Independence, Abigail Adams remained on the family farm in Braintree, Massachusetts earning a livelihood to keep the family going. She did all the "feminine" tasks and took care of all the chores her husband would have done if he had been home.

Abigail Adams, quite a writer, penned over two thousand letters which survive today. Through her letters, we see a woman who was not submissive. She urged John to "remember the ladies" in the organization of the new nation. "Do not put such unlimited power in the hands of the Husbands. If particular care and attention is not paid to the Ladies, we are determined to foment a Rebellion, and will not hold ourselves bound by any Laws in which we have no voice, or Representation."

Abigail Adams was such an outspoken and politically astute woman that when, John Adams, was president, the press called her Mrs. President. It wasn't a compliment. They meant she was overstepping her bounds as a woman by venturing into what they believed should be exclusively male territory: the politics of a new nation.

Nearly one hundred years later when the legal system of this country unfairly restricted women, women took action and pushed for equitable change. Abigail Duniway fought for the right for women to vote. She learned first-hand the unfairness of being a legal nonentity when her husband's decisions led to the family losing their farm. Her husband was later disabled, and she became the primary breadwinner.

Encouraged by her husband that things would not improve until women had the right to vote, she lectured throughout the Northwest. She was once challenged by a man who said, "I have often known a hen to try to crow, but I've never known one to succeed at it yet." Duniway replied, "I once saw a rooster try to set, and he made a failure, too."[11]

Successful Modern Women

Historical women made strides that gave us many of the opportunities we have today. The stories of today's women, both ordinary and well known, can also inspire us to reach beyond our own previous boundaries. As you read these stories, notice the recurrence of the step of dream which we have already discussed. Also look for examples of the steps of discovery, design, development, and diligence that we will address in the remainder of the book.

Ann Richards

Full of charisma, humor and determination, Ann Richards was the first woman governor of Texas in more than 50 years. She was born Dorothy Ann Willis in a small Texas town, the daughter of a truck driver and a home-maker. Ann related how her father encouraged her to test her limits: "He always told me I could do anything I wanted to do if I was willing to work hard enough."[12] She believed him, even believing she could fly like her favorite heroine. "I thought I was Wonder Woman. She had that magic lariat that she could throw out, and it would hold her up. I used to take a rope, throw it out, and jump off the garage."[13]

Ann dreamed of making a difference in the world. By accident, she began to design her dream. Her husband dabbled in politics but had grown tired of it. When Austin Democrats asked him to run for Travis County commissioner, he turned them down, but encouraged Ann to run.

Ann debated running for the office. Did she have what it took? Examining her skills, Ann realized she had shown promise as long ago as high school. In preparing for and winning writing and speech competitions, she had discovered and developed her talent for the power of a good story. This skill would prove invaluable in campaigns. She had already won campaigns while still in high school. She represented her school and later all of Texas at Girl's State, a mock government session designed to teach girls how government works.

Ann's other skills included a teacher's certificate. The perspective Ann's teaching experience gave her into the education system allowed her to make positive changes when she became governor.

Ann developed leadership skills and political awareness as an active volunteer in many organizations including the National Dallas Democratic Women's group, serving as president at one time. She helped organize the Dallas Committee for Peaceful Integration and the local chapter of the National Association for the Advancement of Colored People.

Realizing that she had the skills, loved the challenge and believed she could make a difference, Ann made her decision: "Yes, I will run for county commissioner." She won. Modeling herself after Eleanor Roosevelt, her lifelong hero, Ann achieved significant accomplishments in the office of county commissioner. They included introducing more human services to Travis County, such as an infant-parent training program for families with Downs Syndrome children, a rape crisis center, and a foundation for women's resources. Ann was named Woman of the Year by the Texas Women's Political Caucus.

Her design was working well, but Ann discovered she had personal development work to do. In spite of her public recognition and achievements, she was privately suffering. She had begun to drink socially, then more heavily, and did not recognize her drinking as a problem. Eventually her family and friends confronted her. Feeling betrayed and angry, she stormed out of the "intervention." After a cooling-off period, however, she realized the love and guts it took for her family to confront her. She finally agreed that the drinking had gotten out of hand. She checked into a rehabilitation center, began her recovery and has not had a drink since.

Her recovery from alcoholism was a struggle, but Ann's optimism and determination led her to believe that the experience was "probably the best program for living, for looking at life, that I could ever have gotten. And because that was such a positive influence, I really can't look on it as a failure or disappointment. It was just a very difficult time."[14]

Just when she was building a stronger life through her recovery, the issue of alcoholism came back to haunt her. When she ran for state treasurer, her opponents used it against her as a campaign issue. She was also accused of not having the qualifications for the job, since she did not have a financial or economic background. Embracing the

~ ~

conflicts, she replied to opponents: "I raised a family and ran a household."[15] Contrary to prevailing opinion, she knew that managing a household requires management skills including economic and financial considerations. Persevering through that nasty campaign, Ann was elected state treasurer.

As treasurer, she proved she had economic and financial talents. In a sleepy department renowned for preserving the status quo, she searched for ways to improve quality and shook things up. By reducing the time required to deposit checks from 36 hours to 90 minutes, she earned the state of Texas millions of dollars in extra interest on the deposits. She also hired a diverse team for her staff in the treasurer's office and introduced flexible work schedules.

In 1990, Ann achieved another goal in her design when she ran for governor. Although she won both the primary and the general election by very small margins, she was very popular with the people of Texas. Ann's design included an ambitious legislative agenda. Steven D. Wolens, a Democratic state representative from Dallas, explained her popularity this way: "She's not only hands-on, she gets her hands dirty. No governor has done that in a long time. That's why she was able to set the agenda."[16]

Her first term completed, Ann ran again. Caught in the turbulence of the 1994 elections, Ann was defeated to the disappointment of many devoted fans.

You can be sure she will continue to work toward improving the world. According to the author of the book *Women in Power:* "Richards has the capacity to turn failures into positives. That ability lessens the personal risk because even when she loses, she believes that good things can happen."[17] In her diligence step, she is measuring her success against her standards, and no one else's. To continue pursuing her dream, she has many options with which to design a dynamic future.

Even without the demands of the governor's office, Ann has a full schedule, which has included a trip to Beijing to the International Women's Conference. She continues to design her path to her dream. She believes the hardest question "is knowing what you want. It's not doing it. Once you know, you can accomplish it because there are a lot of people who will help you do it."[18]

Cathy Guisewite

Finding her dream by chance, Cathy Guisewite, creator of the comic strip *Cathy,* discovered that her self-doubt was a marketable commodity. Sounding just like her cartoon character, Cathy says, "Anything is possible if you listen to your mother."[19]

First working in advertising as a writer for television commercials, Cathy bloomed in her career but her love life withered. Discouraged and lonely, filled with self-doubt she poured out her frustrated feelings in her diary. "One night, instead of just writing about it, I drew a stick figure of what I looked like sitting there writing these depressing things and eating everything in the kitchen."[20]

She sent the drawings to her mother, and soon was doing this frequently. Cathy discovered that her mother loved the drawings and believed the cartoons were good enough to be published. Taking a development step for Cathy, her mom researched comic strip syndicates and sent her a list of potential markets. The next development step, sending the cartoons to the syndicates, was up to Cathy. Cathy resisted sending in the cartoons, since they were so personal and not particularly flattering. However, faced with the choice of sending them in herself, or having her mother do it, Cathy sent samples to the syndicates.

When Universal Press Syndicate received her samples, they immediately did what happens very rarely: they signed a contract with her. She had sent them a strip for which they had been looking — one that contemplated the real life of a single working woman.[21] Lee Salem, the managing editor of Universal Press Syndicate explained their decision: "We felt that Cathy the character was real. We were struck by the honesty of her sentiments."[22]

Cathy discovered that her talent for capturing her self-doubt lightheartedly had universal appeal — and one needed in the cartoon market. "Cathy is really my point of view on the world, and it's the only point of view I've got."[23] It was just that point of view, and the ability to express humorously the foibles of her life, that was Cathy's key to her success.

The comic strip *Cathy* first appeared in newspapers in 1976. Since then, many women have been comforted by a character not too different from themselves. "Different comic strips have different functions," says Cathy. "Mine is — especially for women — to let them feel they are not alone."[24] Besides that, she offers a brief respite from daily troubles. Cathy's dream is now to bring hope to women. She said: "I think my job is to offer a couple minutes of relief during the day."[25]

Cathy's success has been legendary. In a World Almanac and Book of Facts poll, editors of daily newspapers across the country selected Cathy as one of "America's Twenty Five Most Influential Women" in 1984 and 1986.

Living her dream life, Cathy says: "It's a great career because it's a wonderful way of expressing yourself."[26]

Caryn Johnson

The dismal New York City project housed Caryn Johnson, but it never felt like home. Plagued with trouble in school, she longed to belong but she felt so different from all the other children. "I must be retarded," she thought. "Perhaps if I could perform on stage, the kids would like me." She remembered the fun of participating in the children's theater program at the Hudson Guild at age eight. She dreamed: "When I grow up, I will be a great actress."

"Yeah, right," she thought as a teen when drugs offered an easier solace. Deciding school was not the place for her, Caryn dropped out. By age seventeen, she was married with a baby. Her difficult life went from bad to worse when her marriage fell apart and she endured the humiliation of living on welfare for seven years. Her dream, however, had not died. Caryn discovered the cause for her troubles in school: dyslexia. With renewed courage, she designed a plan to lead herself out of welfare and into her dream of being an actress.

Her talents and skills were perhaps hidden, but with work, could be developed. Struggling to feed and clothe herself and her daughter, she pursued parts in the local theater productions and earned extra money working at odd jobs such as bricklaying and as a cosmetician in a mortuary. She developed further as one of the founding members of the San Diego Repertory Theater and later various improvisational troupes. About this time, she began to earn enough to support herself. Joyous, she framed her Medi-cal card to remind herself of her accomplishment.

As her performing skills developed, Caryn created a show with many characterizations. One profile is of a nine-year-old girl who yearns to replace her kinky black hair with blond hair because she believes only blondes can be on the "Love Boat." Another profile is of a Ph.D. in literature who is a junkie on unemployment. Caryn put these vignettes together into a one-hour show that played across the U. S. and Europe. This show led to a break she had not planned: producer Mike Nichols came to see her show.

Impressed with her talent, Nichols brought her act to Broadway's Lyceum Theater. Nichols described her as "one part Elaine May, one part Groucho Marx, one part Ruth Draper, one part Richard Pryor, and five parts never seen before."[27] Her show continued to receive rave reviews and enough credibility that Steven Speilberg offered her the part in the movie version of *The Color Purple* for which she was nominated for an Oscar.

Now one of today's highest paid actresses, Whoopi Goldberg has created the common ground with others that she longed for as young Caryn Johnson in the housing project. "I believe I'm here for a reason. And I think a little bit of the reason is to throw little torches out to the next step to lead people through the dark."[28]

Jill Griffin

As early as the fourth grade, Jill Griffin's instincts told her that she was going to be career-focused. Her father, a manager for the local utility company in their small North Carolina town, introduced her to the world of business early. Before "Take Our Daughters to Work Day" was invented, he took Jill to lunch with visiting executives. Jill sensed the excitement of the business world.

Many years later as an adult searching her past to identify her strong points, Jill remembered her speaking skills, how she had won a 4H speech contest and second place in the state in the United Nations Peace Contest. Her prize, $750, had seemed like a ransom to sixteen-year-old Jill and even better was the thrill of delivering the speech in Washington, D.C. She also remembered her writing skills: in her senior year, she had won $200 in a writing contest.

Jill earned a B.A. and an M.B.A. in Marketing from the University of South Carolina. In her second year of college, she added real world experience to academic achievement as the advertising manager for the university newspaper. She managed a sales force of seven who broke all the university records for revenue generated, number of pages of advertising, and sales increases.

Armed with her M.B.A. and her sales achievements, Jill designed a job-hunting strategy to land her first prestigious position. She interviewed job recruiters who came to campus and others who would see her, believing that the more questions she answered, the better she would be at handling interviews. Her desired result: the best job.

Jill showed interviewers the statistics from her record-breaking college newspaper sales force saying, "Here's what I can do." They loved the tangible sales evidence and she got seven job offers. Choosing a position as a marketing assistant with R.J. Reynolds in Winston/Salem, North Carolina, Jill began in the brand management division. Those were great days for her. "It was like I had died and gone to heaven." Learning fast, she recalled how much she loved the work and that for her first three years she hated to see Fridays.

"It was the perfect place for me. I was an enthusiastic upstart on a specific training track. I worked like a Trojan and I got rewarded for it."

Jill also discovered that she had a great talent for observing what was going on. "I'm not the first person out

~ ~

of the gate," she said. "If I can see how someone else does
it, I will use it. I understood what got valued in that environment and I tried to deliver to that value." Jill recalled
how she had wanted to excel at her work. To shine in a
group of overachievers took tremendous effort. She
recalled, "I was willing to pay the price. It was what I liked.
I didn't even want any distractions in my life."

Jill remembered that all through her professional
career she had designed ways to achieve her goals. To move
ahead, she set her sights on the next step and planned how
she could get there. She asked for information to help her
proceed.

She once went into her boss's office and confidently
told him that she planned to get the brand manager's slot
within a certain time frame. Telling him her goal took guts.
He might reply that she was not likely to get the job. She
gambled on her belief that the company didn't want to lose
her. Holding her breath waiting for him to respond, she
knew she would have to live with his answer. She began to
breathe again when he said, "What is your time table?"
Actually, Jill hadn't determined the time table yet, so she
had to think it up quickly. To not put too much pressure on
him, Jill chose a date that allowed for a generous schedule.
He told her that he thought she would make it. She did.

Promoted more quickly than any marketing assistant
before her, Jill actually beat the time table that she had given
her manager and was the first woman to achieve the position
of senior brand manager for the Winston brand.

Jill's first six years set the stage for the next step in her
design. By the sixth year, Jill knew it was time to leave the
company. The demanding nature of her job had begun to
take a toll. She was concerned about her health and was
burned out.

She still dreamed of excelling in business and expanding her skills. She realized that she had not been using her entrepreneurial spirit and excellent selling skills to the fullest. So, she began looking for a sales manager position outside the Fortune 100. Jill saw a job advertised in the *Wall Street Journal* for a marketing and sales director in a start-up hotel company. She phoned. The interviewer told Jill he wasn't interested. She had, after all, come from a tobacco company and relocation expenses would be necessary. Jill boldly told him that he was not going to find anybody better and not to decide before he talked to her. He decided to arrange an interview and eventually hired her.

Elated with her success in landing the position, Jill didn't see the down times coming. She knew she was burned out from her tobacco company job, but she never banked on the demanding nature of this new position. "It was like stepping out of the frying pan into the fire." To make matters worse, she discovered that an alcoholic manager was looking for ways to ensure that her department wouldn't succeed.

A year of struggle — overcoming burnout — was in store for Jill when she decided to leave the job, but she recovered physically enough to design a new plan. She started a business around her preferences: speaking, training, and marketing.

Even in the early days of her speaking business, development steps led Jill to create products for her clients. "My instincts sent me in the direction of developing products. Now today, I can use all those." After several years, Jill wrote *Customer Loyalty,* a well-received book that went to a second printing after only a few months. The success of her book led to many more speaking and consulting engagements.

Born out of disappointments and the examination of her priorities, Jill's new career design hit the target. Reflecting on her life, Jill said, "I've got a great career. Every day brings new challenges." She discovered that even a devastating experience such as her ill-fated job in the start-up company can give you a gift you were never expecting. Today Jill observes, "I love what I do. If I won the lottery, I would do the same thing."

To determine if you are on the right path, Jill believes the litmus test is an affirmative answer to the question "Would you being doing the same thing if you didn't have to?"

To find your right path, Jill advises, "Listen to your instincts and be true to those instincts. That will send you where you need to go."

Barb Schwarz

Although she had vowed to never worry, Barb was finding it challenging to keep her promise. Her real estate career was floundering and paying the bills became an ordeal. She had left a comfortable position as a headhunter for the real estate industry, when a real estate broker challenged her. "Why aren't you in real estate? You'd be great." Barb gave him all the logical reasons why she couldn't do that. "Sounds to me like you're procrastinating," he told her. Barb, with her characteristic energy, decided he was right. Though she never saw the man again, he changed her life by challenging her assumptions.

She launched into selling houses. Now, she was thinking the man had been wrong, and that she had made a big mistake.

"Take action, Barb," she told herself. So she examined

her past to discover clues on how to proceed.

With degrees in Music Education and Interior Design, Barb taught for five years before her daughter was born. Then she wanted to be with her baby, so she operated a design studio out of her home for five years. Doing this, she developed skills in education and design.

Now pondering how to improve her real estate business, she realized that she needed to educate sellers about design issues. She knew that a visually-appealing product created top-dollar sales. Barb also realized how hard it was for her, and other realtors, to tell sellers that no one would buy their house because of the kitty litter box smell or the onion residue odor in the kitchen. She determined to come up with ways to educate the sellers without offending them.

To do that, Barb introduced two concepts which had never been done in the real estate industry: *Staging a Home*[29] and the *Career Book.*[30] Using her design background, Barb created the *Staging a Home* program, teaching her clients how to make their homes attractive and therefore sellable.

Barb developed the *Career Book* by capitalizing on a concept she had developed early in her life. As a child, she had built a scrap book and put all her awards and mementos in it. She used the scrapbook concept for her students when she was teaching. She created one for each of her students. Barb took the same concept, named it the *Career Book ,* and personalized it for real estate. She could now show sellers other homes attractively presented. "I'm an inventor," Barb realized. "I love it! Things come to me!" (Everything Barb says has an exclamation point!)

Her design had the effect she wanted. With these new concepts, sellers and buyers flocked in. Realtors started asking her, "What are you doing?" So Barb started giving classes. Her background in education paid off again. Early in her life, Barb had shown a talent for speaking, though she had long forgotten it. She had won the highest award for speaking in her high school and had loved singing in college. Now, she discovered that her participation in all the programs, plays and operettas during college helped to prepare her for speaking programs.

Soon, Barb began to be asked, "Would you teach my whole company what you taught me?" and, "Would you come to our city to do it?" She discovered her concepts had wide appeal, and she designed her next goal.

In 1985 she and her husband decided they would test the market for public seminars. They developed a brochure, sending it to realtors in five nearby cities. Burning the midnight oil, they developed the products that were necessary for the success of the programs. All their hard work paid off. The first seminar turned a profit, even with the modest turnout of 29 people. By her fourth seminar, Barb drew a crowd of 176.

Today, a large part of her business is in the binder manufacturing business that helps many types of professionals create their own portfolio to use for their personal marketing.

Barb won the "Consumer Education Product of the Year" award for her video that realtors can show their clients about staging their homes. Barb has written two books and recently toured with Barnes and Noble. She is working on a PBS television show.

But all work and no play is not good for the spirit, and Barb's design now includes home time and time with the flowers and trees. Knowing that she has to take time to think, she says, "I don't want to be 'Barbara Do Do.' I want to be 'Barbara Be Be.'"

Barb's troubles early in her real estate career led her to the path that has designed her dream life. "I just kept searching for the answers. You have to be open to what's next and stay in a state of thanksgiving. Keep pushing to discover more." Those early days were tough, but Barb found something inside herself that would not let her give up. Now Barb doesn't have to struggle to not worry. She realized, "I believe everything is perfect and there are no mistakes. We just have to open our eyes and see it."

Barb's advice to you as you design your path: "Do what you want to do. There is a reason your heart is pulling you in a new direction."

Karen Sheridan

Folding clothes as she watched the television, Karen Sheridan noticed the interviewer was talking to Marilyn French, author of *The Woman's Room.* "Hey, that's the book I read," Karen thought as she watched. Married for nearly 17 years with two children, Karen still had not achieved the life outcome she inherited from her Mormon upbringing in Bountiful, Utah. She had valiantly tried to be what she was taught she was supposed to be: a wife and a mother and happy. She was a wife and a mother, but she had the nagging feeling that she had more in her. It's not that she hadn't made attempts at expanding her horizons over the years. When her daughter was 18 months old, Karen wanted to go to school but her husband wouldn't give her the money. "You've made your bed, now lie in it," he told her.

"Women have zero status in the Mormon church," stated Karen. "I was born with a spirit that said this isn't okay for you."

~ ~

Motivated by what she heard in the television interview and what she had read in French's book, Karen decided to get a job. Her husband took it as a joke. Nevertheless, Karen reviewed her history to discover her strengths and talents.

She remembered how she loved to read and to lie on the grass creating things out of the clouds. As a girl, she had the idea that she was born to do something great.

She studied sociology in college dreaming of getting her master's degree and teaching. Looking back on those times, she realized that achievement was important to her even though her college years were interrupted by marriage and the births of her daughter and son.

"No time like the present," Karen told herself as she put on her black suit and went downtown to interview every Tuesday, Wednesday, and Thursday. She recalled, "Here I was, a suburban housewife, going around to companies. I had a blast! It was such fun to get to talk to people." She decided that she wanted a position that paid $25,000 and started getting job offers, but she was very picky about deciding.

Finally Karen interviewed for a position as a manager for a security law firm. She didn't even know what securities were, but she was offered $24,000 a year and took the job.

Karen's mettle was tested one day when a lawyer came in and, like a machine gun, rattled off, "Take a look at this company. Find out how many preferred shares, how many common shares, and how many phantom shares there are. What would be the dilution if everyone converted? What would the capitalization of the company look like?" Karen watched his back as he disappeared down the hall.

With her heart in her throat, Karen locked herself in a room and started going through the request word by word.

~ ~

She figured it all out, along with the numbers and then called her husband to help her figure out the percentages. By 4:00 p.m., she had it done.

That experience gave her a boost. Karen thought, "If I can do that, I can do anything. I felt so confident. I knew I could learn what everyone else knew. We think the information isn't available to us, but we can learn it."

While Karen's design was going according to plan in the career arena, her relationship with her husband deteriorated. In trying hard to make her marriage work, Karen approached her marriage by not allowing herself to see what she saw and not feel what she felt. "I always felt there was something wrong with me. I did a lot of pretending." She didn't feel at liberty to say, "No. This isn't right. That's not okay." After she had worked for six months, Karen's husband left. He wanted dinner on the table when he got home. He told her, "If you want to live life in the fast lane, you can live it by yourself." When her husband left, Karen determined not to pretend any more.

Continuing to pursue her career, Karen dreamed of becoming an expert on blue sky laws. She wanted to know it all. She married her second husband and got her degree in communication. Life was full and Karen was ready for more.

Her next step took her to New York. At age 19, Karen had seen the movie *Breakfast at Tiffany's.* She fell in love with the idea of living in New York, so Karen designed her dream to include a position in New York. She found that position at Alliance Capital — one of the world's largest capital management organizations — with a coveted job as vice-president and a large five-figure salary. Thinking she had found her dream job, Karen was disappointed when changes at the top brought about a different operating philosophy than the one she had been drawn to when she was hired. Undiscouraged, Karen moved on to the Bank of New York as a vice-president, working with high net worth individuals as an estate planning consultant and investment advisor.

She had been with Bank of New York for one and a half years when she fell and broke her leg. Laid up, she returned to Oregon. Soon she was offered a position as vice-president of corporate with a huge drugstore chain. Karen set up the new department communications.

Although she was promoted after six months and stayed for two years, times were difficult once again. Karen reported, "They didn't like me and I never figured out the politics."

One example of her difficulties was when the president said to her, "You know, Karen, you're not nearly as well liked as you think you are." Continually putting her down, this man, who elevated himself by denigrating others, never suggested specific steps for improvement, but he liked Karen's ideas enough to plagiarize them. Frequently, she would bring up an idea and ten minutes later, the president would bring up that idea as if it were his own. He would goad her with such comments as "Your hair looks like shit today." Rather than confront the rude criticism, Karen changed the subject. Sexually harassed for as long as she worked at the company, she endured innuendo, crude jokes and slaps on the behind. She pretended that it was okay.

One day, her boss promoted his daughter. Karen could see the writing on the wall, but she was in the midst of a divorce and not in a financial position to quit. Deliberately, she allowed herself to be fired. The severance package gave her the opportunity to design a new dream.

"I am never going to be in this position again," Karen

~ ~

promised herself. "I'm not doing that again." With her background from the financial services industry, including her stints on Wall Street, Karen realized that she had a vast knowledge of money management that she could share with women. She recognized that women have many issues with money including being afraid to invest.

"We all fear what we don't know," said Karen. Her goal is to make sure that women know about money. The mission of her successful company, Money Mystique, is to be the premier provider of money management education for women so they can use their finances to support their life goals. "Women believe they have no power. They don't realize life is a result of choices. I want to help them do it consciously."

Karen has designed a path supportive of who she is, and believes that her life experiences contributed to her life today. Those experiences led her to the purpose of teaching women how to become financially independent. From those difficult early days as a submissive wife, to her lessons on Wall Street, she is now ready to be who she is.

Gail Raben

Gail Raben's dream has helped empower women to pursue success by helping them overcome internal and external obstacles. She discovered her dream little by little, developing it as she went along.

After earning her degree in social work, she worked at the St. Louis Women's Counseling Center which offered alternative counseling for women. This center was the prototype for the first battered women's shelter. To help clients she learned about the requirements of the EEOC (Equal Employment Opportunity Commission). Her reputa-

~ ~

tion led several companies to consult with her because they had received EEOC complaints. Mediating between the women and the companies, Gail helped resolve many situations without formal lawsuits being filed. Seen as an expert because of her experience in bridging the gap between management and employees, her empowerment work expanded from those first actions.

In the late seventies, Gail started a management consulting company whose mission was to move women up the corporate ladder in Fortune 100 companies. She helped companies write and implement Affirmative Action plans and began to work with individual women. Spending a year with each woman, she would coach her and help design her development plan to move up within the corporation. What elation Gail felt when one of her clients became the first female vice-president in the chemical industry!

Her reputation thriving, Gail headed many major projects. One company had twelve hundred employees and four plants in different parts of the country. Gail helped employees learn to appreciate the value of individual differences which resulted in teams working as cohesive units. Given free rein by management to empower the employees, Gail met with them monthly. She helped them develop a plan to end racial tension, resolving and eliminating racial issues. The team succeeded in eliminating injuries on the job, a bonus from the project the company did not expect.

In another project, Gail designed a plan to balance both the positions and the numbers of men and women in the company. This company had 45,000 employees divided into teams of 250 employees. In the two-year project, Gail taught the employees to empower each other. The plan required that all the employees take a leadership role and

~ ~

come up with the solutions. People with up to a high school education were in front of executives making presentations.

Gail wrote a leadership program for women for another client. It was a mini-M.B.A. program consisting of eleven weeks of classes, three full days per week. Because they were spending so many hours out of the office, the women had to empower their workers to accomplish their assignments while they were gone. The course ran the gamut from negotiation to finance to accounting to personal image projection. The benefit to the company: increased profit levels from increased employee productivity. Following the project, profit levels reached all-time highs.

Men within the company were impressed — and jealous. "How come we never get attention like that," they complained. "You will when women are on parity," management replied and eventually, they did.

Ready to design a new dream, Gail moved to Austin, Texas. She started the Women's Project, which was dedicated to empowering women. "Women want a lot of things. Whether they are willing to take action is a different story." The Women's Project taught women how to take action to convert their wishes into reality. As Gail began this venture, a newspaper ran an article about the mission of the Women's Project. That one article generated 300 calls from interested women.

At the Women's Project, women met twice a month for interactive workshops on leadership, communication skills, and empowerment for women. They were given Homeplay (no homework at this project!) assignments to continue the learning. Women who had never before worked for pay got jobs. One woman who never before earned more than $30,000 publicly committed to making $40,000. She got it.

~ ~

"If you came," Gail said, "The Women's Project worked. It cost $35 a year to join. It was extremely well received."

Throughout this book you will find many other examples of women pursuing their dreams and overcoming the challenges they have faced. All these women show us that we are only as limited as we allow ourselves to be. Whatever your dream is, you can discover it, design a path, take the steps to develop it, and follow up with diligence.

Chapter Three
Discovery

~ ~

"You can live a lifetime and, at the end of it, know more about other people than you know about yourself."

— Beryl Markham

Before you can begin to design the goals necessary to accomplish your dream, you must know where you are starting. When I work with companies on strategic planning, we examine all the factors that influence the business. We look at influences which are both internal and external to the company. Internal factors include the skills of the employees, the processes of the company, the financial situation, the type of work the company does. External factors include the environment, government regulations, situations in the geographical location of the company and competition.

Similarly, in the Discovery step of escaping the Venus trap, you need to take a close look at the important aspects of your life.

Your personal talents and skills are the raw materials you bring to your life. What are your strengths? What are your weaknesses? Where do you have opportunities? What threats might affect the quality of your life and the pursuit of your dream? What do you like and what do you despise? You may be challenged to recognize your talents. We have not been encouraged to notice how talented and capable we are. Nevertheless, we have many personal talents which can help us pursue our goals. We also have skills to help us manage, or perhaps eliminate, day-to-day details which bog us down and prevent us from applying our resources.

Identify Your Strengths

"Whenever I dwell for any length of time on my own shortcomings, they gradually begin to seem mild, harmless, rather engaging little things, not at all like the staring defects in other people's character."

— Margaret Halsey

As part of the discovery step, you must identify your strengths, weaknesses, and opportunities and threats that may affect your goals. Get together a group of friends whom you can trust, and who would also like to pursue their dreams, in a meeting to identify individual strengths. Use these brainstorming rules: Quantity, not quality. Eliminate critical comments during these sessions. Hitchhike on each other's ideas.

Brainstorm your strengths and weaknesses. Look at

~ ~

any opportunities you can see in your future. Also, consider
if there are any threats to your career or relationships
looming.

Another part of discovery is reviewing your personal
history, and your personal preferences. Take the time to
complete the following statements. Share your responses
with your friends:

My biggest achievement in my life has been ...

If I could redo one aspect of my career I would ...

If I had to state what are the two most important things
    to me about my family, I would say ...

If I had to state what the two most important things are
    to me about my work, I would say ...

My greatest satisfaction is ...

My biggest irritation is ...

If my boss could change me, he would suggest ...

If I could change something about my family, I would
    change ...

If I could change something about my organization, I
    would change ...

If I had the power to change myself, I would change ...

After you have taken a look at yourself, look at the
influence your family has had on your life. Has your family
been a strength or a weakness? Does your family life
present opportunities for you, or threats?

Sometimes, our families have encouraged us. Jane Tait
was successful in the corporate business world for many
years, but her dream, to own her own business, was influenced by her father. He used to drive her to school in
another town because he felt the school in the town where
the family lived was not good enough. The ride to school
went past a lumber yard which was run by a woman whose
father had died. Jane's dad told her, "If she can run her

father's lumber yard, you could do it. You could run your own business."

Years later, his prophecy came true. Jane now owns her own consulting company, Development Systems Corporation, which specializes in training front-line employees in such fundamental skills as literacy.

If your family has not encouraged you, don't be discouraged. In the design step, you will design your support system to encourage and empower yourself.

Your Personal Universe

Another way to explore your resources is to look at your personal universe. Try this exercise adapted from *More Games Trainers Play,* by Edward E. Scannell and John W. Newstrom.[31] This exercise taps the power of picturing your life non-verbally.

Each of us is the center of her own universe. We filter, act on, translate, accept or reject people, information, and ideas based on how we feel, think or respond to their influence on our life/universe.

Draw your personal universe, focusing on both your family and the time you spend on the job. Picture your world and all its facets. Draw the universe using the guidelines listed. Art is not the key. Gut level feelings and thoughts are. Read and do each step *in order* before moving onto the next step.

1. On a large piece of paper, and using colors (crayons or markers), place a circle in the center of the paper to represent you. Write your name in the circle.
2. In the space around you, draw and label other circles to represent people or things that affect you.

~ ~

The size of the circles, and the distance from you indicate the strength of the impact that person or thing has on you. For example: a very large circle, or a circle placed very close to you indicates a great deal of impact. A small circle, or one on the periphery of your "universe" indicates less of an impact.

3. Choose another color.

4. Next to each circle affecting you, place a "+" and/or a "-" to indicate whether the impact is positive or negative (good or bad). Some circles may have only one symbol, while others may have both. The size of the symbol will indicate the strength of the positive or negative influence. Example: If a circle has a strong positive influence, and a minor, though irritating, negative influence, you would place a large "+" and a small "-" next to that circle.

5. Now, pick another color you have not used before.

6. Draw arrows between you and the circles affecting you to indicate that the influence exerted is growing or diminishing. For example: If you have recently changed location, and are now geographically separated from your administrator, the influence he or she exerts over your universe is probably diminishing. You would draw the arrow pointing *away* from you. If a circle has an influence in your universe that is growing, or expanding, the arrow would be drawn pointing toward you. Some arrows may point in both directions.

7. Now that you have drawn your universe, you might want to consider the following"

~ ~

   a. Have you forgotten someone or something?
   b. Look at the arrows you drew. Do the arrows
      that move toward you stop at the edge of your
      circle, inside your circle, or do they pass
      through the circle? How are the arrows
      shaped? Are they long, short, straight, or do
      they have hooks, curves, and kinks in them?
      Why?
   c. Use a pencil or pen, and divide your paper into
      quarters. Are certain circles of influence
      located more in one quadrant than the others?
      Are the circles clustered together or spread
      out?
   d. Are any of the circles bigger than your circle?
      Do any of the circles touch or overlap your
      circle?
   e. Are there additional factors you would like to
      show that were not in the instructions? If so,
      make up a symbol and apply it! If you have a
      marker with a color you haven't used yet,
      that's even better. Use it.
   f. Now that you have experimented with your
      personal universe how does it look and feel to
      you, right now?

   Some issues should be apparent. Pictorially, you have
been able to see the opportunities to improve or enhance
your universe.
   Record the opportunities in your universe. This will aid
you in getting a firmer grasp of what you want and how to
attain it. Should you desire to pursue these opportunities in
the future, this information will be helpful. Be sure to label
the universe being written about as current or future.

~ ~

Next discover the influence that patterns have on your life.

Chapter Four
Patterns of Our Society

~ ~

It is best to learn as we go, not go as we have learned.

— Leslie Jeanne Sahler

Have you heard this riddle? A father and his son were in a car accident. The father was killed. The son was critically injured and taken to the emergency room. The surgeon came in and said, "I can't operate on him. He's my son." How could that be? (Before you read further, try to guess.) Chances are nearly ten out of ten that the reader (unless you've heard the story before) cannot recognize that the surgeon is the boy's mother. Why not?

We are accustomed to thinking that the average doctor, particularly a surgeon, is a male. While we know that women can be doctors and surgeons, our minds block the idea of a woman being the surgeon, particularly if she is a mother.

~ ~

To live the life we want, we must notice the social patterns which we have swallowed. Patterns are beliefs that are below our consciousness, and unless we consciously try to discover them, they remain unconscious. Unexamined patterns prevent us from living a life expressive of who we really are, because they lead us down mental paths that close off options which would otherwise be attractive to us.

Natalie Goldberg, author of *Writing Down the Bones* and *Wild Mind,* wanted to be a writer but she had no idea that women could be writers. She wrote:

> I don't even think that I thought of [the poets she admired] as male. They were writers, that's all … I wasn't so much intimidated by these male writers as I was unconsciously accepting a structure: Men wrote, women didn't. It was like someone telling you can't walk in snow. You believe them and then one day you put on your rubber boots and go out and pretty soon you have crossed a large field. What opened up the writing world to me was feminism. Women could write! They could walk in snow. You're kidding! They can? Why I'm a woman! I'll do it. I never thought there was a rule that women couldn't; there was just no perception that they could, no vision of possibility.[32]

Patterns are important to us as humans. We use them every day. We learn that items with four legs, a seat and a back are chairs. We can depend on being able to sit in them. We use patterns to be able to find the key to the house on a chain of ten keys.

Not only are patterns important to us, we learn them very easily. I can get my audiences to buy into a pattern in less than one minute. I say, "How do you spell spot?" They easily spell S-P-O-T. Then I ask, what do you do at a green

~ ~

light? Every audience I try this on says STOP. When I say, "No," they laugh because they realize that what they expected to be right was not. Try this one on your friends, too. This is an example of a pattern that we accept easily and with minimal consequences other than a laugh.

You don't have to accept the patterns you have been given. When my daughter was a very small girl, I tried to speed the dressing process by asking her if she would like to wear the pink or the yellow outfit. I expected her to buy into my pattern. She didn't! Her answer was always the purple outfit! She didn't buy into the pattern, and you can make the same type of choice.

However, all of us have bought into patterns without realizing it. I heard the pattern: do you want to be a teacher or a nurse? I chose teacher. I wanted to say actress. But my mother said that you couldn't make any money being an actress and so I chose teacher. I put off choosing teaching for a time, but I finally succumbed. I hated teaching. The pattern was not a useful one for me. When I became aware of the pattern, I was free to choose another option.

One particularly destructive pattern we have learned is the "Life is Contest" pattern.

The "Life is Contest" Pattern

Growing up in our society, you learn early that "Life is Contest." Some folks are winners, some are losers and some occupy varying ranks in between. You try to "win" the contest of life by pursuing achievements of all kinds. However, you don't start on a level playing field. You learn from an early age how our society assigns value. Each of us is a combination of attributes. Some attributes are "winners" by society's standards: being male, white, thin,

~ ~

rich, and young. Some attributes are less valued: being female, of color, fat, poor, and old. The pattern leads you to believe your personal value, not only your rank in society, is dependent on your attributes.

It is this pattern that causes both women and men so many problems in relationships, both personal and professional. The following paragraphs define the pattern and give examples of it. To be able to come up with good strategies for improving personal and professional relationships, we need a good description of the problem first. Sometimes, understanding the problem is all that it takes to solve the problem. The solution comes almost automatically. Also, you must be aware that there is a problem before you can decide to change it. A vague uneasiness may suggest that a problem exists. The description and definition of the problem is the first step to finding solutions.

In our society white males are on the top of the hierarchy and have the advantage in "Life is Contest." Because society has decided that male and white is the best, white males have the most power. Women and people of color are subordinate. However, men are not the problem. They have bought into the pattern at a very high price. The problem is the pattern of "Life is Contest." The pattern of our entire society is to rank people based on many characteristics. This feels completely natural to us. For instance, who is better, someone who is thin or someone who is fat? Who is better, someone who is young or old? Who is better, someone who is smart or someone who is dumb? Who is better, the woman who won Miss America, or the one who came in 35th? The entire concept of better or worse, superior and inferior, deserving and undeserving, when applied to people, is based on "Life is Contest." All the "isms" we face in our society, including sexism, racism,

~ ~

ageism, and others, result from the "Life is Contest" pattern.

The "Life is Contest" pattern also defines areas of competition for people based on their attributes. Women have been prevented from entering certain arenas of life because of their gender. People of color have been prevented from entering certain arenas of life because of their race.

The "Life is Contest" pattern has allowed slavery to exist, as well as the ownership of women and children. By wars, we determine who will own the land. By corporate takeovers, we determine who will run a company.

In the "Life is Contest" pattern, status is determined by power, specifically the power to establish and enforce domination. Relationships are based on the idea that someone has to be "in charge," "in control," or "on top." The "in control" position must be enforced.

The "Life is Contest" pattern hinders your success personally and as a professional woman because it leaves out the possibility of win-win situations. The "Life is Contest" pattern means that one person must win at the expense of another or others. If others believe that the only way you can win is if they lose, they certainly will fight to make sure they don't lose.

By recognizing this pattern and other patterns which you have bought into, you open up many more options for our lives.

Examples of the "Life is Contest" Pattern

Examples of the "Life is Contest" pattern abound in the business world. The hierarchical structure of businesses and the military have been based on this pattern. Management has been dominant and it is no accident that women have been admitted to the managerial ranks only slowly.

When I served on the board of directors of a chamber of commerce, I observed numerous examples of the "Life is Contest" pattern. Like most chambers of commerce throughout the United States, the majority of members were male. Out of twenty-five board members, three were women. Even the most inane male members of the board were granted more time to talk than the women. The third year I was on the board only one of six nominees to the board of directors of the chamber was a woman. Women represented the bulk of the committee chairs and to this day do the bulk of the volunteer work. Only three women have been the chair of the board in twenty years. The staff of the chamber is all female — except the president and two account executives.

When a new president for the chamber was needed, women were hardly viewed as viable candidates. Out of 500 applicants, five candidates made the short list. Only one was a woman. When the selection committee was considering the candidates, the discussions assumed that the president would be a man. One woman on the committee said, "You know the president could be a woman." Responding to that, another member of the committee, an attorney, said: "Yeah, that wouldn't be all bad. We wouldn't have to pay a woman as much."

A woman, attending one of my seminars, told me about having been in a work group of only females. The women tried to out-dress each other. She believed women were more competitive than men. She felt that in a comparable male environment that kind of competition did not exist. These women were demonstrating the "Life is Contest" pattern though the arena of competition was severely limited. They were demonstrating that when career advancement is not an arena of competition, often we opt for whatever arena of competition we can devise.

You may have heard men talk about the mystery of women and how they cannot figure women out. Simone de Beauvoir said that men use the "mystery" as an excuse for men to *not* try to figure women out. Using Freud's question "What do women want?" the male asker never waits to hear an answer. De Beauvoir said that male privilege allows men not to answer the question. Women and other unprivileged *have* to know about men as a matter of self-preservation. Only the privileged can roll their eyes and say, "What a mystery."

Freud, definitely steeped with men as the norm, defined the biased (and ludicrous) concept of penis envy. Simone de Beauvoir contended that girls do not want the flap of flesh, but what they do want is the privilege which males have in our society. She says that boys also experience envy, but in different ways. Boys envy the ability of women to procreate. Boys also envy girls their relationship with their mother which boys are shamed into ending earlier in life. (For a hilarious review of the extreme bias of Freud, see Gloria Steinem's *Moving Beyond Words.)*

Costs of the "Life is Contest" Pattern

Aside from pantyhose, the "Life is Contest" pattern costs our society dearly. Domination requires constant and never-ending vigilance. The vigilance takes a lot of energy away from creative effort or the task at hand. An "on-top" position is never secure. To maintain the "on-top" position, the dominator must not value the unique contributions of others. The pattern of thinking goes, "If everyone's contri-

~ ~

butions are valuable, what will keep me on top?" The irony is that in today's business place, that kind of domination provides only a false sense of security. Domination interferes with productivity and may lead the dominators to lose their positions of authority.

What is the cost of being a dominator? You have to pretend you are always right, and are afraid of being found out. You have to hide your true self.

What are the costs of the "Life is Contest" pattern to men? They must deny their feelings of vulnerability, their weaker moments. They always must be in control. They must put up a shield which prevents intimacy even when they would like to be intimate. Denying feelings results in a loss of sensitivity and the never-ending concern about maintaining strength. Trying to be strong all the time — and especially stronger than everyone else — shuts down openness to other feelings. Pretended strength requires being dominant. True strength does not need to dominate to prove it is strong.

Dominance also requires hatred and prejudice. "Hatred and prejudice," said David Aronson, editor of *Teaching Tolerance* magazine, "are tools of the subconscious that ease the feeling of insecurity by offering the illusion of superiority."[33]

This observation describes what happens in the "Life is Contest" pattern with respect to the relationship between men and women. Jokes demeaning women, sexual harassment, reinforcing narrow roles by censure, these are all tools of the subconscious that ease the feeling of insecurity by offering the illusion of superiority. We have bought into the belief that we must be superior or we are worthless in the "Life is Contest" pattern of relationships. Unfortunately for the dominator, insecurity continues to undermine self

~ ~

image because examples that contradict the idea of superiority constantly arise.

It seems obvious that there are more responsible ways to achieve emotional security. They include:

- learning to respect yourself for your own individuality;
- believing that you have the right to make mistakes; and
- believing that you don't have to be superior.

"Life is Contest" creates many more problems for the dominated. Being dominated results in the suppression or atrophy of talents. The creative systems are shut down due to lack of use and lack of appreciation and acknowledgment. Resentment develops because the dominated feel unappreciated and suppressed. People submit to domination for many reasons, most frequently because they don't realize there are other options. Unfortunately, submission cripples potential and creativity goes untapped. In a conducive environment, everyone contributes much more and power is released to create a better world.

Another obvious problem with the "Life is Contest" pattern is that no human (whether man or woman) likes to be dominated. When dominated, they cease thinking for the good of the group (organization or family) and begin thinking of ways to escape (daydreaming, leaving the organization, etc.)

The "Life is Contest" pattern prevents women from achieving equality. When your view of the world is based on the belief that there are only two sorts of folks, the dominator and the dominated, it is not easy to believe that women could have rights without men losing theirs. You can be sure that anyone threatened with losing power and privilege will use every weapon (literal and figurative) to

~ ~

prevent that from happening.

As women in business, we face the fact that management has been masculine for many years. We take note that women who have become successful in management match the stereotypical male role better than the stereotypical female role. Because of the narrow definition our society accepts of what is female, women are often forced to choose between the masculine and feminine model. The question for the aspiring women then becomes: Do I act like a manager or do I act feminine? What is called assertive in a man may be called aggressive in a woman.

The double bind that this creates for women is that to "win" the "Life is Contest" pattern, they must match the set of characteristics that is assigned by society to the category of "feminine." "Good" women match the feminine characteristics. "Bad" or "inferior" women have the masculine characteristics. To win in the manager category, a woman must match society's characteristics of manager, which, not surprisingly, are the same as masculine.

The "Life is Contest" pattern suppresses diversity because of fear. When everyone is judged by the same standards (and the standards are invented to prefer a certain group), value results from matching those standards, not from each individual's unique, and uniquely valuable, attributes. Accepting diversity threatens the core of the "Life is Contest" pattern because if diversity is valued, superiority is meaningless. Those on top in the "Life is Contest" pattern may resist the idea that people are only different, not better, because they feel they will be losing their edge. Even those not on top may resist the idea of everyone being inherently valuable because they may lose what little edge they feel they have.

The "Life is Contest" pattern also perpetuates dishonesty. If you are afraid that you will be punished (fired, beat up, demoted) for speaking your true mind, you are not likely to be honest. Bosses get insulated from the truth because no one is brave enough to be honest. It follows that if you derive your self-worth from being stronger than a woman, you are not likely to be honest when you are feeling weak. And it also follows that if you are afraid your husband will leave you if you speak your mind, and as a woman you feel personally defined by your husband, you are not likely to speak up.

Relationships based on the "Life is Contest" pattern deteriorate because of the lack of honesty. If you cannot share truths with each other, then what you are sharing is deceit. Complete honesty may never be achieved, but the closer to honesty you become, the better the relationship.

It takes courage and more personal integrity to tell the truth since we are trained that we are good or bad based on whether we measure up to external standards. The truth is that we are good because of our uniqueness and our differentness — not because of our sameness. The more we can value diversity in our society, the better we will become. Business will be stronger because of the synergy of new and different ideas. Families will be stronger because we can begin to share who we really are, rather than live behind the masks of whom we should be.

Riane Eisler discussed a concept similar to the "Life is Contest" pattern in her classic work, *The Chalice and the Blade.* Calling it the dominator pattern, she explored the concept in terms of human relationships. The societies which most of us know are based on the dominator, or "Life is Contest" pattern. As we have explored, this pattern bases relationships on hierarchy (who is better than whom) and society prescribes who is on top of the hierarchy. We assume that the structure of our society is the only way to structure relationships.

Other societies have been structured in other ways. Eisler studied ancient societies where the evidence led her to believe that relationships were equal. In those societies, difference was not equated with inferiority or superiority. These societies based relationships on linking rather than ranking. Humans lived as partners without violence or dominance. Eisler called this the partnership pattern. I call it the "Life is Connection" pattern.

About 4,000 years ago, invaders from the peripheral areas of our globe conquered the peace-loving, partnership people. The social model for much of the world changed to a model of domination, or "Life is Contest."

"Life is Connection" Pattern

To avoid all the problems associated with the "Life is Contest" pattern, we need to develop the belief that "Life is Connection." The "Life is Connection" pattern bases relationships on networks of linking, living and working together as a team. The "Life is Connection" pattern recognizes that none of us exists independently. Any assumption that limits one of us will limit us all. What is harmful for any of us is also harmful for us all. We cannot put down women without losing potential for the world.

The "Life is Connection" pattern was described by Riane Eisler as "... a partnership society in which neither half of humanity is ranked over the other and diversity is not equated with inferiority or superiority."[34] The "Life is Connection" pattern recognizes that women are as normal as men. Or, as one cynic wrote, that may be setting our sights too low. Men do not define normality any more than women do. What *is* normal is diversity.

A "Life is Connection" pattern furthers the progress of everyone. It does not require success by stepping *on* someone else. When we are connected, we join forces to solve problems, meet opportunities, and create visions together without the wasted effort of maintaining a hierarchy.

Power is only harmful in the context of a "Life is Contest" pattern, where power is used to take things (both tangible and intangible) away from the weaker/dominated. Power in this model is used to force the will of the dominator over the dominated. In the context of the "Life is Connection" pattern, power is applied to accomplish goals. To achieve this kind of power, one must have access to supplies, information and support. Access to information and support is much easier in a "Life is Connection" relationship.

The following table compares the "Life is Contest" and "Life is Connection" patterns.

"LIFE IS CONTEST"	"LIFE IS CONNECTION"
Value is based on external standards	Each person is inherently valuable
If you win, I must lose	We can all win
Power by intimidation	Power by cooperation
Some people are better than others	Each person is uniquely wonderful
There is only one right way	There are many options
Conflict is negative	Conflict is information
Fear of losing position	Position is irrelevant
We must not make mistakes	Mistakes are our teachers
Difference is bad	Differences are resources
Top down communication only	Open two-way communication

~ ~

Avoid negative consequences	Pursue joy
Dishonesty prevails	Honesty prevails
Conserving	Discovering
Only the chosen few deserve dignity	Each person deserves dignity

Fostering the "Life is Connection" Pattern

"It's a great satisfaction knowing that for a
brief point in time you made a difference."
— *Irene Natividad*

One woman asked me how to approach the subject of
the "Life is Contest" pattern with her primarily male work
group. She was concerned that her work group would not be
receptive to discussing the concept. In a high-trust, egalitarian environment, a frank discussion of the concept is
enlightening to everyone. However, most of us are in envi-
ronments in which trust is seriously limited, and we may
need to use another approach. A talented facilitator can
guide a discussion of the subject within the work group.
Even if the "Life is Contest" pattern is not discussed
directly, it is useful to us to realize the underlying currents
of what is going on.

Applying the "Life is Connection" pattern to the
example above, the woman could talk to her group about
what they want to accomplish. Focusing on what you wish
to accomplish directs your efforts to achieve specific goals.
She could discuss those behaviors which are interfering
with each individual's personal achievement as well as
those of the group. When we believe that we are connected,
our actions are more likely to consider the consequences for
each individual within the group.

Intra-team competition on any level hurts the team.

Effort is wasted when team members concentrate on outdoing one another, rather than accomplishing the mission of the team. Ill will is created by setting up a situation within the team in which you have winners and losers. Limiting women to "feminine" roles is like tying the women's feet. Tying the feet of part of the team is a sure prescription for the destruction of the team.

Here are some strategies for approaching relationships from a "Life is Connection" orientation. Look for other strategies as you explore the "Life is Connection" pattern in your daily activities.

- Use quiet time in your life to continually ask yourself what do I want to happen in this situation. Use the question: "In the best possible of all worlds, what would happen?" Then explore options of how to create a situation as close to your ideal as possible.

- Be honest and brave enough to express what you want and how you feel even if it may meet with the disapproval of others.

- Recognize that if you do not match the characteristics prescribed by society that you may be challenged. Use your internal guide to determine if you are taking right action, rather than the judgement of others.

- In "Life is Connection," you must be connected to yourself first, and then to others. Ask yourself if you are proceeding as you want to proceed, or are you assuming that you have to lose in any interaction.

- Remain open to the perceptions of others. Really listen when someone describes his or her point of view. Listening does not mean you will have to

~ ~

change or that you will "lose." By listening
carefully, you have more information for developing a creative win-win solution to any problem.

- Remind yourself in any situation that there are
  many creative solutions that result in more than one
  winner. It is possible for everyone to win. Ask
  yourself: "How can we work this out so that
  everyone wins?" Remember that there is a huge
  difference between a solution where everyone wins
  and the traditional view of compromise. Everyone
  minimizes how much they lose in compromise. In
  a "Life is Connection" solution, everyone
  maximizes how much they win without creating
  losses for anyone.

- Notice when you are worrying about whether you
  are better than someone else. Not only is this
  wasted energy, but it is destructive to yourself as
  well as to the relationship with the other person.
  Any comparison is a trap.

- Observe instances when there appears to be a
  selection process that leaves out one of the genders.
  Make a conscious effort to include both genders.
  For instance, in a chamber of commerce board of
  directors, if there are twenty-five men and three
  women, in the next selection process, actively look
  for qualified women to add. Don't perpetuate the
  problem by neglecting to think of women as candidates in the next election. In addition, remember to
  think of men for committee work.

- When you notice a woman being cut off from
  talking, you can interject, "I wanted to hear the rest
  of Mary's statement." If someone attempts to
  interrupt you, rather than deciding that you are

boring and worthy of being interrupted, say, "I would like to hear your point immediately after I finish my point." Then, continue until you are finished.

- Ask yourself if you have different standards for women than for men. As I mentioned, I am frequently told that women are more competitive than men. Is this true or is it that we expect women to not be competitive, therefore when they are it is more noticeable? (See the reverse test below.)

- When a problem occurs, remind yourself that there are many solutions to any situation. Take the time to brainstorm those solutions, after seeking input from everyone affected. In a business setting, this may require a meeting to explore options. In a family setting, conduct a family meeting and seek input from every family member.

Understanding and noticing these patterns of behavior and our assumptions helps us build partnerships which are beneficial to us and to our team.

The Reverse Test

"A man has to be called Joe McCarthy to be called ruthless. All a woman has to do is put you on hold."

— Marlo Thomas

Another way to check out the patterns that hinder women's success is to use the reverse test. If a situation can be reversed, then it is probably not biased. If it cannot be reversed, we need to take a second look.

The reverse test can show us where the "Life is Contest" pattern is operating. If you can reverse something, there is no power inequity. If you cannot reverse it, there is probably a power inequity and perhaps a perceived value inequity.

Women in history used the reverse test to make points about the right to vote. The following hilarious rendition was written by Alice Duer Miller, a novelist and poet who lived from 1874 to 1942. She wrote the following in 1915, five years before the Nineteenth Amendment gave women the right to vote:[35]

Why We Don't Want Men to Vote

1. Because man's place is in the army.
2. Because no really manly man wants to settle any question otherwise than by fighting about it.
3. Because if men should adopt peaceable methods women will no longer look up at them.
4. Because men will lose their charm if they step out of their natural sphere and interest themselves in other matters than feats of arms, uniforms and drums.
5. Because men are too emotional to vote. Their conduct at baseball games and political conventions shows this, while their innate tendency to appeal to force renders them unfit for government.

(Copyright 1974 The New York Times Company.)

The reverse test is still useful today. I recently read a series of articles in *Cosmopolitan* about the women's movement. Each article devoted several paragraphs to why feminism did not mean that women had to hate men. What would that be like in reverse? Think about an article in *Gentleman's Quarterly* on the men's movement. Would *GQ* spend much ink on how the men's movement didn't mean men had to hate women? It doesn't seem likely. The dynamic operating results in articles on the women's movement addressing male concerns when articles on the men's movement don't address the concerns of women.

Several years ago, the reverse test helped me make a decision that changed the probability of success in a project I was undertaking. After joining the chamber of commerce, I got actively involved in the seminar committee because I wanted to promote my business by giving seminars. I figured that I would have to organize the events to get to speak. The committee chair asked me to head a committee to do a seminar for women entrepreneurs. The Small Business Administration was to cosponsor the event, which we named "The Enterprising Women Conference." After many organizational challenges, the event reached the stage when it was necessary for the seminar committee chair and me to arrange for presentation space. A local college promised us free space in one of the college conference rooms. The man representing the college assured us that he didn't know which room he could put us in, but that we could rest easy: he'd allocate appropriate quarters.

Three weeks before the event, we needed the exact room location to put into the promotional brochure we were designing. We called the man and he informed us he was very sorry that he didn't have a meeting room for us at the college, but that we could stage our event at the associated high school.

I was furious. I asked myself, "Would he have done the same thing to a group of male attorneys who were planning a conference?" I didn't think so. I decided that we wouldn't settle for the crumbs he was throwing. His secondary inferior location wouldn't be suitable. We postponed the event for a month, but when we held the conference, it was housed in one of the city's nicest hotels, and it was a great success. I know we would not have had the same success in an un-airconditioned, aging high school.

Frequently, I present sessions with many women and only a few men. It is interesting that typically the women treat the men with the utmost respect and actually make them the center of attention, giving them more airspace and electing them as leaders of their groups. This is an interesting example of the reverse test. On the other hand, when I've observed a single woman in a group of men, she has not been singled out for preferential treatment. In fact, much research indicates that workplace situations where there are few women but many men are the most likely ones for sexual harassment to occur.

The term "male bashing" doesn't seem to pass the reverse test. Ever heard of someone saying "female bashing?" This is particularly interesting since research shows that one woman is physically abused every six seconds. We don't even have a slur to describe the man who does that.

"Feminist bashing" is commonplace, but I bet you've never read the term in the newspaper or even in a book until now. It only recently has become recognized as bad taste to tell jokes demeaning women. (If it is recognized now. See the story about Ann Humphreys in the section on Speaking Out.)

It is more socially acceptable to criticize women than it is to name discriminations. I watched a "Murphy Brown" episode recently in which she attended a college class that was for women to discuss their abuses. Some of the women described treatment they called abusive that was totally ridiculous. (For instance, one said she was abused because some men were playing football outdoors when she was inside.) Other women who were on the other side of the class said that they hated feminists because the feminists had told them they shouldn't have families and they wanted them. Here were women, instead of deciding what they wanted and needed and pursuing it, were attacking other women because of their attempts to name injustices and improve the world. The anti-feminists were more comfortable attacking women than attacking social conventions that kept them from pursuing their dreams.

Frequently in seminars a woman will come up to me and say that it is the women who are the problem. The media has had a heyday recently insisting that women do not want to call themselves feminists. Even feminists feel more comfortable attacking other women than in attacking the inequities in society. It is socially acceptable to point out all the weaknesses and foibles of women — but it is not socially acceptable to point out the weaknesses and foibles of men.

A recent book is titled *Ten Stupid Things Women Do to Mess up Their Lives*. It is a best seller. Can you imagine men snapping up a book entitled *Ten Stupid Things Men Do to Mess up Their Lives?* Pointing out a mistake made or an injustice perpetrated by a man is tantamount to male bashing. Pointing out the mistakes of women doesn't even seem out of place.

The reverse test is helpful in evaluating things we read. Instructive were two articles on sexual harassment which appeared in the *Wall Street Journal*.[36] One described how the defense attorneys in a sexual harassment case used the sexual lives of the plaintiffs (women) as a defense. They asked the plaintiffs such questions as did they have premarital sex and were they promiscuous. The attorneys suggested that the women welcomed sexual advances from the defendants. The prior sexual activity of the plaintiff was irrelevant to the case. No matter what the plaintiff's activities, the law theoretically protects people from harassment. This was a unique case in which the victim was being tried for the crime that abused them. No other crimes put the victim on trial. What if we reversed the situation, and considered a wealthy man who was mugged as he walked down the street wearing a Rolex watch and gold cuff links? Would the mugger's defense attorney accuse the man of welcoming the attack because he was wearing expensive jewelry? Would the defense attorney ask if the man had been mugged before, suggesting that he liked to be mugged?

Remember to check out patterns you encounter with the reverse test. By noticing the patterns and seeing a situation where reversing doesn't work, you can look for a solution.

Internal Barriers

> "Fortunately analysis is not the only way to resolve inner conflicts. Life itself still remains a very effective therapist."
>
> — *Karen Horney*

One of the worst problems with the "Life is Contest" pattern and the limiting assumptions which are part of it for women, is that we internalize these messages. We become our own worst enemies as we pursue the life of our dreams. We don't acknowledge the part our abilities have played in creating our success. We hang onto outdated beliefs about what we can't do. We put all our efforts into pleasing others, denying to ourselves those activities which please us.

The following sections explore ways to become aware of barriers (both internal and external), overcome them and discover your talents.

Discounting

If you are like many women, you may be slow to recognize your own abilities or you may discount their value. You may think you have succeeded for reasons other than your own talents and merit. We often attribute our success to such factors as luck, easy tasks, other people, charm or hard work. This type of delimiting undermines success by preventing us from acknowledging the skills we have used to create positive results. We succeed once, but don't realize we can succeed repeatedly.

Research has shown that men attribute their success to ability; both men and women in research studies attribute women's successes to luck. If we believe that women succeed only by chance, by extension we also believe that women are incapable of creating success.

Another way in which we discount our abilities is to insist to ourselves that the task was easy. This idea results from the conviction that women do not have many skills. Therefore, women must not be able to accomplish difficult tasks. By extension, the logic goes: if a woman did accomplish the task, it must have been easy.

Another form of discounting is for women to think their success was created by the efforts of others. I once complimented a volunteer committee chair on the excellent job she had done. "Oh, it wasn't me," she said. "I had a wonderful committee who did it." It is true that we cannot accomplish great successes alone. Some of the biggest failures I have ever seen have resulted because one person tried to be a hero and accomplish a major task solo. However, if we have the skill to get others to help us and to support our causes, that does not mean that the success was created by them. That means we can mobilize resources to accomplish our goals.

We may attribute our success to charm. As women, we feel free to acknowledge charm because it is consistent with the traditional female role. But charm will only take us so far. Without intelligence, talent, and skill, charm will only serve to make people think we are charming, not take us closer to success. Besides, in today's world, and with many people, charm is an asset that is difficult to come by. If you are charming that is a great skill in itself.

Women often attribute success to hard work alone, again failing to give themselves honest credit for their skills. In one research study, men and women managers were asked to account for their success. Men felt that hard work and ability were equally important. Women attributed their success to hard work. The problem with attributing success to hard work alone is that it leaves out one important ingredient: skill. No matter how hard you work, you will not accomplish much without skill. Oxen work hard but they don't accomplish goals. They merely accomplish the goals of others.

Discounting keeps us from experiencing ourselves as competent and talented. We do not pay attention to what we did well and how we did it. When we realize that our skills and abilities created our successes, it helps us continue through hard times when our actions do not produce the results we want.

You can easily see examples of discounting in professional meetings. One woman I know is beautiful and tall with Rubenesque features. She has a face that is pleasant to look at with no sharp angles or unpleasant features. She has stunning silver hair with never a single one out of place. I have never heard her utter a sentence which I thought was stupid and she often makes comments I think are quite perceptive.

At a recent board meeting, she had been waiting politely for her turn to talk. She raised her hand just slightly above her shoulder and when the president turned to her, in her discussion, she started a statement with the words, "Maybe I am naive."

She wasn't naive. She was intelligent, capable, and insightful. Why should she prejudice her listeners with a tentative statement when it was not true? Don't frame your remarks with a judgmental statement about yourself. Never ever do that. Try not to do it in your head. Listen to yourself when you talk to yourself. If you are being judgmental, stop it. Don't ever say to yourself, "You idiot, there you go again, talking so ugly to yourself." Be gentle with yourself and don't do it!

We don't need internal judgements such as those we get externally. We are going to see ads where women are depicted as stupid. We are going to see ads putting down mothers-in-law. Let's agree to not do that to ourselves. Try being sweet to yourself for a day. See how you feel. Then, try being very judgmental about your every action. See how you feel.

With practice, you can improve your own self-confidence just by refusing to undermine your own self-confidence. Actually, think about how creative you can be about telling yourself why you can't do things! Use that same creativity in the pursuit of your goals.

~ ~

Learned Helplessness

Another internal barrier to success is learned helplessness. A researcher named Seligman experimented on dogs. Although his methods may have been questionable as to humaneness, his results have valuable conclusions for women trying to succeed in today's business world.

Seligman placed some dogs in a box in which they could not get out. He then subjected them to electric shocks. Then, he placed the dogs in another box in which they could leap over a barrier to get away from the shocks. The dogs which had been shocked previously just laid down and took the new shocks docilely. They did not attempt to get away. Dogs which had not been shocked soon learned to jump over the barrier.

In a way women have been conditioned to lie down and docilely accept their "less than" status. As girls get older, they go from being self-confident persons to tentative women. As girls reach adolescence, they become less confident and more uncertain in offering their opinions. In one study, girls at age 12 used hesitant expressions such as "I don't know" 21 times. By age 14, these terms cropped up 135 times. It appears that girls learn not to express their opinions directly by this age. This is a form of learned helplessness. As women, hesitations affect our level of success.

The lesson for women in the business world is that we need to continuously reevaluate our previous limitations. Actions which did not succeed in the past may succeed now because the world, or we, has changed. Things we couldn't do in the past, we can do now. Sometimes, we may feel and act helpless when in fact we aren't.

Before adolescence, girls do better than boys in school and on achievement tests. After adolescence, boys catch up.

~ ~

Is it because girls get less intelligent? It doesn't seem likely. Perhaps many girls are like I was. When I was in high school, I tried hard to not do better than the boys on tests so the boys would like me. I purposely made lower grades.

Look at the beliefs underlying this strategy of deliberately reducing grades. It demonstrates the belief that boys were so important that they must be pleased. Also, boys are pleased when they are superior to girls. It was my responsibility to please boys. It was so important for boys to like me that I had to pretend to be less than I was. Unfortunately, the price I paid still did not give me the result I wanted.

The bad news is that the boys didn't like me anyway! What a rotten bargain. My grades were good but they could have been great if I had not been looking for love in all the wrong places. We sometimes adopt the conscious or unconscious belief that we must please everyone. Pleasing everyone is an impossible task. By trying to please everyone, you so bind your actions that you often do nothing to achieve your own goals. By thinking of everyone else first, you neglect your internal self, your own map of what you want and what you were created to do.

When you begin to pursue your goals, approval from your friends and family may disappear. You may want them to acknowledge your progress, and they may resist the change. You must not depend on others for confirmation of your success. Look inside yourself for approval. If you must please everyone, you cannot take the necessary steps to learn what you need to learn. Those who are too frightened to reach out will not like it when you do. Accept this and continue on your path.

It is also important to find supportive others who can help you along your path. Support is quite different from approval. Many organizations are available to help you network and gain both information and emotional support to continue pursuing your dream. However, no one else can tell you what is right for you. You still are the final source of defining what is best for you.

Don't let internal barriers shift your attention away from your goals. Don't allow yourself to get stuck in an outmoded version of the past. Ask yourself how have you succeeded in the past and how can you create the results you want now.

Lack of Confidence

Frequently, our capabilities are not reflected in our confidence. We feel like imposters. When I ask women if they have ever experienced lack of confidence, they often respond, "Have I ever not experienced lack of confidence?"

Lack of confidence faces many professional women. *Working Woman Magazine* wrote about the "Imposter Syndrome." The Imposter Syndrome faces many executive women who think they will be found out. They fear that they do not have the skills that they need and that they are merely good at keeping up the pretense of being capable. Many of us have experienced feeling as if we are going to be found out at any moment.

Catherine Fyock, although talented and highly successful as an author, told of having dreams about being naked. Psychologists suggest that dreams of being naked are reflections of fears of incapability. Catherine said her dream was expressing her fear that in writing her book she was going to be documenting her incompetence.

Sometimes other women seem as if they are totally confident. Mary Moore, a successful consultant, seems very confident. I had lunch with her one day when I was not feeling confident, so I asked her about being confident. She said that doing what she wanted to be doing in her life was part of what contributed to her confidence. She described her sense of mission and how her actions were aligned with it. She said she didn't know where her path would lead but that she was sure she was preparing for the next step. She also said that her previous job steps: a teacher, and then sales and management, had led her to her present position as a business owner. She said that her husband was very supportive and encouraged her in what she does.

When I finished the lunch, all my muscles felt tense and sore. About half way through lunch, I also got a tremendous headache. I told her several stories about myself which depicted struggles or failures in my eyes. I worried that she would think I was incompetent. Then I thought, well, surely she has had similar instances in which she felt inadequate, but she didn't share those. I think I wanted her to tell me she struggled too. I noticed that I seemed to focus on my failures, while she focused on her successes.

Mary focuses on what she does right, rather than on her shortcomings. It is partly Mary's success in business that led to her confidence but I suspect it is even more than that. She seems single-minded in her focus on her successes, and she also focuses strongly on her goals. She has many projects she can pursue and is excited by all the possibilities.

Another woman, Irene Levitt, is a successful consultant on handwriting analysis. I asked her how she got started in the field. She told me she had applied for a job, and was sure she would get it. She went for the final interview, talked to the board; they loved her and she waited outside to hear that she had gotten the job. A man came out and told her she didn't get the job. He said that she crossed her t's

~ ~

low on the stem and that although the board had really liked her, they felt that the low crosses on the t's indicated that she had low self-confidence. Irene told me that although she hadn't realized it, her self-esteem was low at the time.

She went to the library and started researching hand-writing analysis. Looking back at old college papers, Irene discovered that when she was younger, she had crossed her t's at the top of the stem. That was before she dropped out of college to put her husband through law school. Leaving college, she went to work and also raised her children. During that time, she subordinated her needs to those of her family. Her self-esteem had suffered. Losing the job offer was the catalyst for Irene to begin the process of under-standing herself and thereby rebuilding her sense of self-esteem. She investigated graphotherapy which is devoted to changing the way a person writes, and by extension, the way she or he thinks. Every night for two weeks, she wrote the line 30 times: "Take time to think." Irene went on to get a master's degree in graphoanalysis, the science of hand-writing analysis, and now helps others improve their lives using graphotherapy.

Building Confidence

"Any mother could perform the jobs of several traffic controllers with ease."
— Lisa Alther

Glenda Graves appears thoroughly confident. Successful in her career, she sells for a hearing aid company. I asked her how she developed her self-confidence. "My mother pushed me to excel. I want to win and I want that recognition. I am very competitive. I make things into a contest even though I am the only competitor. I set a goal and try to reach it before my deadline." For Glenda and many others, confidence results from the goal setting process and achieving goals.

Keep in mind that the most confident person you know has days when she feels totally inadequate. In this respect, Glenda observed, "I go through periods when I am not at all confident. I want to sit in the corner and eat worms." One technique you can use to improve your self-confidence is to focus on your successes. The cardinal rule of success is to accentuate the positive and eliminate the negative. While it is frequent that you may run replays of your failures through your mind, you can choose to run replays of your successes. To use this technique, answer these questions:

1. What successes have you had? Write down at least twenty.
2. What do you like about you?
3. What contributions do you make to your work?
4. What contributions do you make to your family?

Every day before you go to bed, write down what you learned from that day and write at least five compliments to yourself.

Notice your relationships. Are you in relationships in which you receive compliments on your efforts (and your existence)? Are you in relationships that undermine your own sense of effectiveness? If your relationships do not support your confidence, you have several options. One is to excuse yourself from the relationship. Another is to ask for what you need in the relationship.

One of the hardest things I ever did in my life was to ask my mother to tell me five things that she liked about me. I felt as though she did not love me. When I told her how I felt, she was completely surprised. "How could you ever think that?" she asked.

I don't know the answer. I guess I just never heard her say what she liked about me. The list of five she gave to me was a surprise. I never knew that she liked the things she described. Ask significant and supportive others what they like about you. You may be surprised too.

Jane Tait tells a story about when she went skiing. While on the ski lift, she noticed those signs that warn skiers to keep their ski tips up. Misreading the sign, Jane accidentally came up with a statement that always boosts her confidence and gives her a smile. She says to herself, "Keep your tits up, shoulders back." Telling herself that makes her smile and reminds her to act confident and self-assured.

Last year, I attended a conference on writing books. One speaker, Jeff Davidson, an author with more than a dozen published books, gave great advice that applies to developing self-confidence. He said that you shouldn't approach a publisher with your hat in your hand, but rather with the attitude that you have something of value to sell and if the publisher wants to buy, great. If your book doesn't appeal to the publisher, that's fine and you can take it elsewhere. That is a great attitude to have about any endeavor you undertake in your life. Say to yourself: Here I am. I am a valuable product. If you like what I have to say, great. If not, fine. I will take my product elsewhere. And *I am still valuable whatever your reaction to me or my product.*

The following observations from Gail Raben, who I introduced earlier, are from a book she is preparing. They are thoughts of great relevance to women.

"Yes, we've made progress, but we must be honest and say today women find themselves still dealing with the

~ ~

same issue we dealt with 20 years ago. Jobs, kids, money, relationships. However, today many women are ready to take a stand on themselves. They are beginning to realize that even though change has occurred, the unspoken promise of that change is not going to be delivered. There are no leaders to look to for answers, there is no coordinated 'movement.' Women individually, are the only ones who can possibly lead their lives in the direction they want to go. Looking to social change to make the difference for women has slowed down our progress because, as we've sadly discovered, giving our power to someone else, or something else, to make it happen never has and never will work. What is needed now is for women themselves to individually create a vision for their future, then come together with other women for support and empowerment and put that vision in action.

"Women need to invent a new future for themselves, individually, and then contribute from their success to promote other women."[37]

~ ~

Chapter Five
Design

~ ~

"Persons who wait for a roast duck to fly into
their mouths must wait a long, long time."
— *An old Chinese proverb*

I'm not sure about how to get a roast duck to fly into
my mouth. However, Ben and Jerry sure do know how to
get their ice cream to fly into our mouths. I think it all
relates to those little pint containers. They are so dear that
you must take several home with you. One is not enough
and you never know what flavors the family will like to eat.
And no one would ever think of eating out of a half-gallon
box or a gallon tub. But those little containers, it hardly
seems worthwhile to waste a bowl to put the contents in.
The ice cream sits in the freezer and says, "Come eat me.
I'm here all alone." And then since the ice cream is sloping
up against the walls of the container, it would be so much
neater if you could clean it off.

~ ~

It is amazing how creative your mind can be when it comes to eating ice cream for very good, rational reasons. Now all you have to do is to apply that same level of creativity to designing your goals — and your success is assured!

Once you have discovered where you want to be (your dream) and where you are with the internal and external landscape of your life, and you have identified your resources, you are ready to begin designing how to get to where you want to be. Now is the time to set goals for your life's work. If you don't have a plan, you become part of someone else's plan. This step takes you through setting goals and objectives leading to the steps necessary for finding your dream. Goals lay the foundation to create your dream. Because you began with your dream, the design of your goals and objectives will make sense in the framework of the big picture of your life.

This top-down approach to goal setting is important. When you begin to set goals you are not setting them in a vacuum. You still have those clothes at the dry cleaners, dirty dishes, children and daily maintenance activities to consider. You still have your relationships to consider. You may be changing the course of your professional career, but it is not likely that you will abandon your present life totally. It is far more likely that you are going to adjust your present life to make room for growth. However, without clarifying what your resources and restraints are, goals will not be nearly as achievable, and they will not make sense in the greater scheme of your life.

The design phase, which takes into consideration your internal and external environment, breaks your dream down into goals. The goals are reduced to objectives. Objectives then become actions you can take on a daily basis.

~ ~

Once you have created your plan, you should begin to act on it. To get a jumpstart ask yourself: "What small step can I take today to move my dreams toward reality?"

Decide What You Want

"You don't get to choose how you're going to die. Or when. You can only decide how you're going to live. Now."

—Joan Baez

What you learned during the discovery step leads directly to your design. Review your written dream. Look at the lists you brainstormed of your strengths and weaknesses, as well as the opportunities and threats facing your life. Look at the descriptions you made of your resources, your growing up environment and your present one. Your design to accomplish your dream will evolve from your discoveries.

In her book, *No More Nice Girl*, Rosemary Agonito says we need to create ourselves.[38] Our job in our lives is not to support others but rather to create ourselves in the process of living. We can't do that if we are doing nothing but responding to the needs of others. We need to be proactive about our lives, rather than reactive—just like successful businesses.

Like many of us, Agonito drifted through her life, because she assumed that the role of wife and mother would be fulfilling to her. She also took on these roles before she analyzed whether she wanted to be a mother and if so at what particular time in her life. Only later, did she realize that her socialization and upbringing led her to buy into the expectation that she would be a wife and mother first, and pursue other activities as a secondary role. Uncertain that she could create her life in the way she wanted it, like many of us, she failed to make a plan to guide her way.

In my own case, I have certainly done my share of drifting through life. Many times I have said, "Well, I really want to be an actress, but I guess I will settle for being an Earth Science teacher." Or, "Well, I really want to be a speaker, but I guess I'll settle for being a consultant." At what point do we stop settling and start going for what we want?

Janet Oglethorpe described her career progression, one that is common for many women. First she studied psychology. It took her seven years to get her undergraduate degree because she alternated working with going to school. She never thought about how she would earn a living with her degree. She is somewhat angry now that no one ever asked her the question, "How will you earn a living with that?"

She says she assumed that she would be supported by a husband and that her parents probably assumed that also. She was accepted into a doctoral program in developmental psychology in a prestigious school, but began to wonder why she was doing it. She noticed that recent doctoral graduates were doing post-doctoral work because they couldn't find jobs. A bike accident which left Janet hospitalized gave her a respite which allowed her to ponder her future. She decided to get her MBA, and then made it her goal to become a college professor (something she had thought would be neat from the time she was 13 years old.) Earning her doctoral degree, she achieved her goal of becoming a college professor. Even now, in spite of her achievements, she still asks herself, "What do I want to be when I grow up?"

~ ~

We all need to be designing what we want to be when we grow up. After determining your dream and discovering your talents, the next step is to decide what you want.

Listen to Yourself

To decide what you want, listen to your emotions. Depression, anger and other emotions are like an answering service. All of these emotions have messages for us. "Hello, what was the message you had for me?" The answer is not always quick to come on the line. We may think, "Oh am I on hold?" We must patiently listen to ourselves to get the answer.

Listen to yourself when you are disturbed. It is hard for me to be honest with people about how I feel if something disturbs me. The biggest struggle and lesson I have learned recently is to pay attention to myself when I am uncomfortable about what someone is doing. To learn to do this has taken much reflection and discovery of what is going on inside me. Once I was at a business meeting of three women in a casual setting. Each of us had one hour on the agenda. During my hour, one woman present kept getting up repeatedly. She kept apologizing and I kept saying, "Oh, it's all right." When I was driving home that night, I realized how angry I was with her that she had spoiled my time to have the undivided attention of everyone during my presentation.

To help you decide what you want to do most with your life, tune in to yourself and examine your memories of the pursuits which have made you the happiest. I noticed that the happiest times in my life were when I was actively involved in creative activities. In the fourth grade, I was putting on plays with my best friend, Rachel Amburguey. In high school, I worked in the drama department. In college,

~ ~

I was exuberant building a vegetable coop. Throwing my energy into an exciting project creates the happiest periods in my life. Conversely, the most miserable times of my life have been those when I was consumed with doing mundane, daily tasks: when life was a blur of spit-up and dirty diapers. We have to use "out-of-the-box thinking" to keep our lives working in the ways we want.

The Critical Inner Voice

Don't listen to your critical inner voice.

There is a creative child inside me which my critical inner voice tries to keep tightly under lock and key. The child tries to get out, but if the critical voice keeps beating her down, she stops creating and instead mopes. It is amazing how persistent are the approaches the critical voice uses to stop the creative process. Even when the rational adult voice attempts to quiet the internal critic, it comes up with zillions of reasons why I should stop what I am doing.

My son, Luke came into my room one day in the middle of my writing. He wanted to talk. I guess he just wanted to be with me for a little while. He said that he wanted to write a science fiction book, but he didn't know how to start. I said that it didn't matter, he could start anywhere and he could figure out the beginning later.

He said, "I don't want to start anywhere. I want to start at the beginning."

I said, "Go ahead and do it." Then I sent him to bed.

About 15 minutes later I went in to check on him. He was sitting in front of his computer writing his science fiction novel! He had the first paragraph done.

"Do you think it's good, Mom?" he asks.

"I think it's great, Luke. You are so creative."

~ ~

I thought, gosh, I hope he doesn't get those internal dragons that kill his creativity as my dragons have done to me. Well, they haven't killed my creativity, but they have certainly gotten in the way.

To get past the critical inner voice ask yourself what you would say to a dear friend to help her drown the voice of pessimism. When I got stuck writing this book, that's what I did.

I realized that if a friend were stuck on her writing project, I would say, "Go ahead, keep working. Some day you will proudly see the results and a book will be published. What a thrill that will be! But right now, just keep going. It doesn't matter if it is perfect. You can make it perfect later. You will figure it out as you go along. Go away critical voice!"

As a matter of fact, you figure out the design for accomplishing your dream as you go along. Sometimes, we get stuck because things don't turn out like we expected. There are very few experiences in our journey which are of life and death import. Most of the things we are really stuck on are just lessons. They are not all that threatening. Every experience, positive or painful, leads us in the direction of bigger and better things.

I have had the good fortune and the good sense to listen to many inspirational speakers and writers. I have been given a helping hand by those who have gone before me and have made a difference in my life by showing me ways around, over, under and through those dragons of defeat. I am grateful for the work of those folks, and I want to help others, who like me, have underestimated their potential.

~ ~

What Would You Do If You Could Do Anything?

"I believe that what a woman resents is not so much giving herself in pieces as giving herself purposelessly."

— *Anne Morrow Lindberg*

Ask yourself what you would do if you could do anything. The answer to this question has helped others create the life of their dreams.

Chris Clarke-Epstein's father was a master salesman. Following in his footsteps, Chris sold real estate, then policies for a small insurance company, then moved to a large insurance company, Blue Cross Blue Shield. At Blue Cross Blue Shield, she sold to companies with 25 to 150 employees.

While she was working at Blue Cross, another salesperson and she went to lunch one day. They began to play "Ain't it Awful" about their jobs. The pay was good. The benefits were good. They said to each other they could be at the company for 10 years doing the same thing. They could hold on for security reasons and let go of what they felt would feed their souls. Then they switched to talking about what they would do if they could do anything they wished. There at the restaurant, they planned an entire business on a place mat, but they didn't start the business then.

Some time later, they got laid off and decided to start the business they designed on a placemat. Chris began the life of her dreams. When she became a speaker, she knew she had found herself. She believes that her earlier positions prepared her for the present. Those experiences gave her material and wisdom to draw on.

Goals

"While others may argue about whether the world ends with a bang or a whimper, I just want to make sure mine doesn't end with a whine."
— *Barbara Gordon*

One day at a swimming pool, I saw two girls making a game of throwing their ponytail holders over their backs and then racing each other to see who could get to the target first. If you watch girls before they are socialized to be passive, they invent and enjoy competitive-type activities. They demonstrate the marvelous desire of the unfettered human spirit to achieve.

Goals can help replace the joy of testing your limits. Goals help you achieve the joy you may remember experiencing as an exuberant young girl. By creating definite goals, you are promising yourself to test your capabilities against an anticipated accomplishment.

Once you have decided what you want, the next step is for you to decide what has to happen for you to get it. Break your desires down into goals that will lead you to your dream.

Why Set Goals Anyway?

Goals help us stop settling for less. Goals get us going for what we want. Goals help us keep our spirits up when we encounter hard times. Also, goals help us measure our progress against what we intended to do. Things happen because you make them happen. Or as Alice in Wonderland said, "If you don't know where you are going, you'll probably wind up some place else."

~ ~

Goals create powerful results. In the famous Harvard University study, one class of graduates was surveyed. They were asked: Do you have written goals? Three percent of the class said yes. Twenty years later, the researchers looked at each graduate's net worth (the value of all of their holdings after subtracting their debts). It turned out the net worth of the 3% exceeded the net worth of the 97%. This provides incredible testimony to the power of goals.

In 1984, Louise Hay set a goal. She wanted to write a book. She determined that she needed to take off two months from her work to accomplish her goal. Even though she was not sure she could make it financially, she took the time off and wrote her book. Published in October 1984, *You Can Heal Your Life* made the *New York Times* self-help paperback best-seller list four years later.[39]

Another woman who has used goals throughout her life is the world famous psychiatrist Elisabeth Kübler-Ross. When she was 15, her father decided that she should come to work for him in his office. She had another dream for herself and told him no. He told her, "If you don't become my office assistant, you can leave the house and become a maid if you prefer that." She left his house, and went to work as a nanny in order to earn the income to pursue her dreams. Elisabeth later said, "I knew that if I started in an office it would ruin my chances. My dream was to be either a doctor or a farmer, and I thought that when you are old your brain doesn't work as well, so you better become a doctor first and then add farming later. Exactly what I am doing now. The ultimate dream was to be a researcher of nature, nature of humankind or anything else that is alive."[40] Elisabeth has made the study of humankind her life's work, setting and meeting many successive goals along the way. She became a physician, later a psychiatrist, and developed

~ ~

the concept of the stages of grief that has helped millions of people deal with those painful experiences. Her book, *On Death and Dying,* is a classic for the helping profession.

Later in life, Elisabeth got her farm and, while continuing to conduct workshops and pursue her other work, she farms as well.

You gain many benefits by setting goals. Like everybody else, you spend much of your time communicating. If you have no goals, you cannot communicate to your family, friends, boss, and co-workers how you wish to spend time and how they can help you. Your significant others won't understand how to help you unless they understand what is important to you.

Without concrete goals, if trivia sidetracks you, you may not realize you're lost. You may go in circles or nowhere at all. Without goals, you won't know when you arrive where you wish to be. With goals, you get the satisfaction of knowing when you've arrived.

Goals give you a target and direction. The specific goal is not as important as the fact that you have set it. You may discover another, even more meaningful, goal as you go. The value of the goals is that they get you on the road.

Achieving goals is fun and creates positive motivation. As Oliver Wendell Holmes said, "The greatest thing in the world is not so much where we are, but in what direction we are moving."

Goals must be challenging and flexible. Goals have a beginning, middle, and end. They help us concentrate on results.

Goals help you control your time. When I knew I wanted to write this book, I gave myself the goal of writing four pages a day. I am at my best in the morning, so I knew I had to block out time early in the day to work on my

~ ~

project. With the goal set, I arranged my calendar in a way that placed me in front of my computer, writing away. I set appointments for meetings and interviews in the afternoon. Without the goal, I might have wasted many great mornings by meeting with people, and ended up in the afternoon without the energy to be creative.

Make Your Goals Bite-Size

A company president with a Ph.D. in psychology wanted to develop a method to insure that new employees would reach optimum performance as quickly as possible. He conducted a study to investigate the best methods to motivate his new unskilled employees. With one group, he set the goals very high, requiring unskilled workers to reach minimum production within 12 weeks. The group reached only 66 percent of standard performance after 14 weeks.

The second (equally unskilled) group was given weekly goals which were programmed to become progressively more ambitious each week. As the level of the employees' proficiency increased, the goals were advanced. At the end of the 12-week study, the second group achieved their goal of reaching the proficiency of a skilled operator.[41]

Setting goals high enough but not out of reach is ideal. Be sure not to set your goals too high or else you may undermine your motivation. How do you learn what is high enough? Experiment! My tendency when I began my business was to dramatically underestimate the difficulty of projects and to think I could accomplish a month's work in a week. With effort, I have now gotten that down to thinking I can do two weeks work in a week!

Especially if you want to balance family with your dreams, set realistic goals which lead to bigger ones. Set

~ ~

small goals at first and when you are cheered on by their successful completion, set slightly higher goals.

Goal-Setting Process

> "A goal is nothing more than a dream with a time limit."
>
> — *Joe Griffith*

Dream
⇓
Goals
⇓
Objectives
⇓
Actions
⇓
Weekly Plan
⇓
Daily Plan

Once you have your dream in mind and have discovered where you are now, break your dream down into manageable chunks. What must you do to make your dream come true? The critical technique of setting goals and objectives starts with long range planning and works to short range. Goals and objectives differ in length of time. The time to achieve a goal may be one to five years. Objectives are more immediate and should be in the one day to one year time-frame.

Goals are statements of intent to create value that enable you to prove you've created it by meeting clear standards of performance. Recognizing this definition, ask

~ ~

yourself what kind of value you intend to create. Who will benefit from the creation of your value? How? When? Where? How can you best demonstrate that you've succeeded in creating this value?

Goals must be written. You will not clarify your goals if they are not written. Goals left in your head change. We forget, we tire; we need written goals to focus on. Write yours down.

It is also important to choose only a few goals at a time. I like the number three. I can keep three goals in my mind at a time and evaluate incoming activities easily with this number. Does a new activity take me toward one of my three goals? If so, I do it. If not, I can decide to postpone it until later.

Break Your Goals Into Small Increments

I once heard Peter Vidmar, an Olympic gold medal gymnast, describe how he prepared to win the Olympics. He said that by working 15 minutes longer each day, he added 91 hours more per year, and got himself ready for the big win at the Olympics. He asked himself when he was tired and not feeling particularly like practicing, "Is my vision still worth working for right now?" He also said how one feels is irrelevant to the task. I think he meant that if you give in or give up when you are feeling down, tired, and just worn out, you will not reach your vision.

I like his thought, but I believe feelings give you important messages with which you can aid your progress. However, you must keep reaching even when you feel overwhelmed and not up to the race. I listen to the message in my feelings, but I don't allow the dragons of defeat lurking in my mind to discourage me.

~ ~

Richard Ott, in his book *Unleashing Productivity,* says that you should not have goals because the deadlines are discouraging and you can't control the speed with which you accomplish something. I don't agree that you shouldn't have goals, but his point about discouragement is worth considering. You can't control the speed of progress. You can decide whether you will allow the rate of your progress to discourage you. My suggestion is: don't!

According to my definition here, goals do not have a deadline. Your objectives will have a deadline, which we will discuss next. With objectives, you choose actions that you can control (such as how many hours you spend on a task.) You can't control the progress, but you can control the actions you take. Goals are much bigger and you may not be able to accurately determine how long something is going to take, particularly if you have not done it before. Goals are intended to be general. You may estimate that you want this to be a one-year goal, or a five-year goal, but the time-frame should be indefinite.

It is possible to use goals to abuse yourself. You could beat yourself up if you fall short of your goal or change your mind. Don't do that. Goals are just a way to get yourself going in a direction that you can learn from. They are the engine that gets you going. Once you are on the road, you can turn off on a detour if you want to see something else along the way. You may turn back to your original goal later, or you may decide to go a different direction altogether. Either way, it's okay. Goals help you get out of the driveway. What you discover along the way is beautiful and wonderful. You don't know what you will discover. That will be your gift.

~ ~

Objectives

"Grain by grain — a loaf; stone upon stone — a palace."

— *George Bernard Shaw*

After deciding on your goals, the next step is to break those goals down into objectives that you can accomplish. Each goal will divide into several, separate objectives.

Characteristics of Smart Objectives

Many business seminars and books develop outlines on how to create "SMART" objectives. The letters in the word SMART stand for good ideas.

S stands for Specific. Objectives must be specific or you will not know when you have accomplished them. For instance, if your goal is to buy a house, what kind of house do you want? If your goal is a new relationship, what specific kind of relationship do you want?

M stands for Measurable. Make your objective measurable in some way. "I will write four pages a day." Or "I will make four phone calls this week." If you can't measure the objective, you won't know if you are succeeding.

A stands for Attainable. Attainable means you can make it happen. You must be able to accomplish the objective. One unattainable objective might be to decide "I will have a baby this year." Another might be "I will be promoted to manager in four months." These objectives are not attainable.

Attainable objectives are "I will stop using birth control this year." Or, "I will prepare myself to be promoted to management by taking the required courses by the end of January."

The major consideration to determine whether an objective is attainable is that you can control what happens. For instance, you can control how many phone calls you make. You cannot control how many sales you make. If you have an historical perspective or enough information to make an informed guess, you can predict the number of sales you will make based on the number of calls it takes to make one sale. However, setting an objective for sales is beyond your control. Set your objective in terms of calls. If you know that making calls leads to sales, then it is a matter of time until your sales will increase if you make the calls.

R stands for Realistic. The realistic part of objectives usually refers to one of two things. One is the schedule you have chosen to accomplish the objective. You can accomplish any objective given enough time. Getting your Ph.D. in three months isn't realistic. Getting it in four years is probably realistic. The second consideration is that it is possible to choose a combination of objectives that isn't realistic. Obtaining your Ph.D., getting married and having two children in four years is probably not realistic.

Sometimes we discover from experience that an objective is not realistic. Once, I gave myself the objective of making 20 prospecting calls per week. I actually accomplished my objective for several weeks. However, soon I discovered that as appointments and business started stacking up, I couldn't keep up the pace and do the important follow through. So I adjusted my objective to a number of calls that was more realistic.

T stands for Time Table. Your objectives need a deadline. It is human nature to procrastinate. We need to build in those deadlines for ourselves. If you say, "Some day I will learn ballet," you can bet money that someday will never come. Deadlines create an urgency that magically helps get things done. Build a deadline into every objective. As you determine your time frame, take into consideration other items and actions on your agenda for the coming week or month.

Converting Your Goals and Objectives into Action Plans

> "It had long since come to my attention that people of accomplishment rarely sat back and let things happen to them. They went out and happened to things."
>
> — *Elinor Smith*

Break your objectives down into tasks that you can actually put on your daily "to do" list. One by one, begin to take the actions necessary to accomplish your objectives.

Your approach to any goal or objective may take many different forms. To generate a lot of great ideas, try this idea that my husband and I use. We go on a walk in a park. While we walk, we brainstorm ideas. Say we need to increase cash flow. We brainstorm ways to accomplish our objective in the short run. We take a micro-cassette recorder and take turns putting the ideas we generate on the tape. By doing this while walking, we have more creativity because of increased blood flow to the brain. Later, we put the ideas down on paper and select the best ones to put into action.

Build in Options

When we view our lives strategically, we should never have only one option. If you have only your job and would be devastated if you were to lose it, you place yourself in too much risk. You may be tempted to accept behavior from others upon whom you depend that you would reject if you had other options. If you are married, and your economic survival depends on your husband, you place yourself in a position of having to take whatever he dishes out. You must always have options for yourself or you are not truly free.

Even if you love the job you presently have, continue networking in other organizations and look for opportunities should your present position deteriorate. Build relationships with other departments within your company so that you could make a lateral move should it become necessary.

If you have options you are not nearly as likely to endure abuse, fearing that if you speak out you will lose your job (or your livelihood). Women with options are not nearly as likely to be battered because they can leave the situation.

Deciding Priorities

"One can never consent to creep when one feels an impulse to soar."
— *Helen Keller*

As we begin to work on our action plans, it is important to understand the concept of important versus urgent. Important tasks lead us to achieving our goals. Urgent tasks must be done immediately, but may not be important in the scheme of our goals. An example might be a phone call from a telephone solicitor hawking a product you are not interested in. The ringing of the phone is urgent, but the call isn't important to your goals. Another might be a television show that is on right now and so you watch it, but you didn't particularly want to see it. Our lives easily fill with urgent tasks, and the important tasks get left undone unless we schedule those important things.

Anne Wilson Schaef described how she designed a life that supported her: "I get a massage almost every week, no matter where I am. I eat a healthy diet, I schedule time alone, and if I get to a point where I feel I need a block of time and I don't have it, I'll cancel. In general I really listen to my body and pay attention to my needs."[42]

Leaving Stuff Out

"Cleaning your house while your kids are still growing is like shoveling the walk before it stops snowing."

— *Phyllis Diller*

One important part of achieving your dreams is figuring out what you can leave out of your busy life. One chore I decided to leave out is doing the laundry. One day I was complaining to an acquaintance about how long it took me to do the laundry, and how the kids, 11 and 13, would put clean clothes back in the hamper just so they didn't have to put the clean, folded clothes in their drawers. She suggested that I let the kids wash their own clothes. I felt like I had found a hundred dollar bill on the sidewalk.

"Yeah, they can do that," I said. Of course, it became something of a test of wills, because the kids just didn't wash their clothes at all. But in some cases I can be very, very patient. I ignored the dirty clothes, even when the kids were wearing them. I prayed they would eventually decide to wash their clothes. They did — and what a relief to release that chore to them.

You get to decide what you spend your time on. Evaluate the benefits and joy you get out of any activity. I met a hair stylist the other day who professed to have hair as curly as I do. Her hair was shoulder length and very straight. I didn't believe her. Since I was a teenager in the sixties, I always longed for straight hair rather than my kinky, curly hair. I have tried to straighten it numerous times with no success. In fact, in high school, I followed the craze of ironing my hair. My hair looked like flat rick-rack. So, I asked the woman, how did she get her hair so straight?

She coached me on how I could make my hair straight, by using a very hot blow dryer and pulling the strands taut. She said she spent an hour blow-drying her hair every day. I spend 10 minutes washing my hair, fluffing it up and letting it air dry. I could choose to add an hour to my grooming every day, but why? It just doesn't seem like I would get commensurate joy out of that.

Don't get me wrong. I am not saying that you should not spend whatever length of time you choose and wear your hair in any style you choose. Spending an hour doing her hair was worth it to the stylist. All I am saying is that if you consciously choose to spend part of your time on any activity, make sure that it has an adequate payoff for you.

Good choices are the essence of setting priorities. Analyze those things that will have the most impact in your life and will bring you the most pleasure. Leave out the tasks that don't make much difference to you, and increase the time spent on the tasks that bring you pleasure. In that way, you have more joy and less grief in your life.

~ ~

Getting Your Team to Do It

"A mother is not a person to lean on but a person to make leaning unnecessary".
— *Dorothy Canfield Fisher*

"There's a lot more to being a woman than being a mother, but there's a hell of a lot more to being a mother than most people suspect."
— *Roseanne Barr*

Part of your design will include how to get the family maintenance activities done. With your family as your team you can enlist their aid in creating time for you to achieve your goals. Depending on their age and abilities get them involved.

Spend time discussing your goals and theirs. Have a family meeting periodically. Discuss as a family what your family dream is. Also discuss what each person's dream is, and how the family can contribute to the accomplishment of each person's goals. In addition to each individual's goals, set goals as a family. Together choose family goals that are exciting.

After setting a family goal ask the question, "How can we make this happen?" If your family wants to vacation in the Rockies next summer, and money is tight, brainstorm together ways to make that happen. If you need more time to spend calling on clients and fixing supper gets in the way, ask for ideas from the family about how to get supper done. Amazingly good ideas come from rather young children, and by the time the children are eight or so, they frequently have better ideas than the adults in the family.

Handling Chores

"My husband and I have figured out a really good
system about the housework: neither one of us does
it."
— Dottie Archibald

Jane Tait got her family to help with the household.
"We all had to help. Otherwise, it wouldn't get done. They
could see the benefits if we worked together." She balanced
her family with her dreams because her family was part of
her dreams. Her husband is a housewife. He does his own
laundry. She does hers. He shops at Sam's. She shops for
minor stuff at the grocery store. They have a cleaning lady,
and each of them takes and pick ups his or her own laundry.

Make your expectations clear before you establish a
relationship. One woman told me she put more conscious
thought into her second marriage than her first. "My expectations were clear from the beginning that I wanted a partnership. We're pretty good at recognizing balance and who
picks up the slack. We keep our expectations clear. We love
to travel so we do as much as we can. We love to cook and
neither of us cares if there is a big mess in the kitchen. The
last person out of bed makes it so we are cheerful either
way. If I have to get up early, then at least he has to make
the bed."

One single woman whose kids were young allowed
them to be responsible for their own rooms. If the door was
closed on a messy room, she didn't care. "I decided that I
could win a limited number of battles. Cleanliness was not
one of those," she observed. To keep the cleanliness to a
manageable level she hired teenage girls, the kid's babysitters, to help clean the house. Mom, kids, and babysitter

would clean together. The babysitters made money. The kids learned how to clean. Mom got time to pursue her goals.

Here's another way to handle the chores. Write a list of all the jobs that have to be done to keep the board of sanitation away. Cut the list into slips of paper. Each person takes the jobs she or he likes the best. Once the jobs everyone likes best are chosen, next have each person take the jobs she or he could tolerate. For the jobs that everyone hates, get everyone to think creatively. Could you hire help for these jobs? Or, so that the burden seems less annoying, could you make a game of it.

At our house, we plan the menus for the week on Sunday. The kids look forward to menu-planning and grocery shopping. We have the agreement that whoever cooks the meal gets to choose the menu for that day. The kids compete for who gets to cook the most! (How I love that!) After we plan the menus we go to the grocery store together. We have our list divided into two parts (one for the left side of the grocery store, and one for the right side). We split up into two teams, one child and one parent per team. Within half an hour we have our groceries bought for the week without creating an undue burden on any one of us. Each one of us also chooses one treat (popsicles, cookies, or snacks) for the week during our trip.

Chapter Six
Limiting Assumptions

~ ~

"Sometimes people want to tell you to act or to be a certain way.... Never limit yourself because of others' limited imagination; never limit others because of your own limited imagination."[43]

— Mae Jemison

Before you can design the life of your dreams, you must know what gets in your way. Assumptions are patterns that you have unconsciously accepted. By examining the assumptions that you may have bought into, you can open many other options for your life. Often the patterns of our society prevent us from noticing information that challenges our accepted beliefs.

Tom Peters, in writing about new ways of doing things, observed: "At some point long ago, somebody invented the wheel, and you can guess how the early users were portrayed: The other guys stood around and said, 'What a sissy! Real men carry things on their backs!'" It never entered Peters' mind that the inventors of the wheel (and fire and numerous other civilization-enhancing discoveries) were likely to be women. Many experts believe that women probably did invent the wheel and discover fire. Yet, you often hear about "the man who discovered fire." If it was a man who discovered fire, why did women get stuck with the cooking?

Peters does have some good advice though he may not be taking his own: "The old American attitude, to own everything and control everything, does not work any more." He adds: "Take your most cherished assumptions. Don't modify them a little bit. Throw them out. And that goes for my theories, too."

Assumptions frequently take the form of stereotypes. Simone de Beauvoir, in her book *The Second Sex,* discusses an interesting fact about stereotypes. When a woman does not fit the stereotype of "femininity," it is the woman who is wrong, not the definition of "femininity." It is also true of masculinity.

Riane Eisler explored the problem of male stereotypes in the *Chalice and the Blade.* Eisler says:

> The underlying problem is not men as a sex. The root of the problem lies in a social system in which the power of the Blade is idealized — in which both men and women are taught to equate true masculinity with violence and dominance and to see men who do not conform to this idea as 'too soft' or 'effeminate.'[44]

In the business world, we are restrained by many unspoken and unexamined assumptions. As women, we are bombarded with books and seminars telling us how to dress and how to behave. We have become convinced that if we just dressed and behaved in the "right" way, (read, the way the author or speaker thinks women should dress and behave) we would achieve levels of success equal to those of our men counterparts. Mark Twain had the best attitude about dress I have read: "Clothes make the man. Naked people have little or no influence in society."

Chris Clarke-Epstein, a successful professional speaker, believes it will never be okay for women to be who they are until we just are who we are. She says, "Gray hair is liberating. To wear it is a visible sign of opting out of the traditional judgment standards. It is a freeing of layers. It says: 'I started accepting myself.'" Chris's hairdresser couldn't understand and kept asking her to color her hair, so she finally changed hairdressers. If we embrace ourselves, it helps us to move beyond.

Learning better communication skills helps, and a polished appearance makes a difference, but many other factors have a more significant impact on the reception we receive in the business world. Such factors include the "Life is Contest" pattern and the assumptions we have learned. This chapter examines many other common assumptions that our society teaches.

Appropriate Feminine and Masculine Behavior

We're immersed in a society which has very strict prescriptions for the behavior of men and women based on their gender. It isn't that men have done this to women. All of us "do" this to women and to ourselves. Our society and our collective beliefs, taught to children and reinforced by our language and the media, create these prescriptions for what men and women should do. The potential of both men and women is limited by assumptions about what men and women can and "should" do. Sure, things are a lot better now than they were in the fifties. Even so, we accept without question many subtle biases and beliefs. We are so used to believing that men are one way and women another that the very thought is invisible to us. We are like the fish who swam through the sea to find the queen fish and asked her, "I've heard of this thing called a sea. But where is it?"

We have absorbed beliefs about what constitutes appropriate feminine and masculine behavior. These beliefs are adopted when we are very young. My daughter came home from the second grade crying that the boys called her bossy. How did children after only seven years of life come to the conclusion that our society prescribes that girls "shouldn't" be bossy? Can you imagine a little boy coming home crying about the same taunt or even any child using that taunt against a boy? Also, why didn't Lea say to herself, "Hey, what's wrong with being bossy?" I told her, "That's okay, Lea. The bosses get paid the most." She dried her tears and smiled. I wondered, "How many women have had similar taunts that prevented them from exercising their autonomy?"

It doesn't get better as we grow up. A female management consultant for a big eight accounting firm was being considered for the position of partner. Although she had brought the firm $40 million in contracts, she was passed over two years in a row and told to cut her hair and wear makeup. She won her discrimination lawsuit against the company, but the amazing thing is that the firm prized its attitude critical of her nonconformity more than it did her obvious value to their bottom line. Because management was blinded by the fact that she did not match the feminine stereotype, they failed to profit from the continued contribution of this very valuable employee.

We may even find the pressure to conform to ingrained biases emanating from ourselves rather than from others. Glenda Graves, successful in physical security sales, found a huge challenge in accepting a role reversal in her marriage. Her husband was looking for a job and Glenda found herself the family's primary breadwinner. The role was uncomfortable for her and she found it challenging to keep it together for her family. "I feel like I've become the standard bearer. I would sometimes like to be by myself and only responsible for myself." A part of her challenge came from her traditional upbringing and her solid beliefs about the contrasting roles of males and females. Glenda admitted that if she were the husband and he were the wife, she would not be so challenged by her shifted responsibilities.

Men and Women Are Different

"There is only one sex.... A man and a woman are so entirely the same thing that one can scarcely understand the subtle reasons for sex distinction with which our minds are filled."
— George Sand

A big deal is made out of the differences between men and women. Are the sexes really all that different? And does it really matter? The problem with the assumption that men and women are different is that it limits many individuals.

There seems to be a conspiracy to maintain a sharp division between men and women. Research studies that don't show a difference between the genders are never published and are thrown out.

John Gray has made a great success telling us how different men and women are in his book *Men Are from*

Mars, Women Are from Venus. According to him, we're so
different it's as if we come from different planets. In reality,
we will never know if men and women are different because
the one thing they have in common is that they are raised
completely differently. The effects of early training cannot
be separated from biology. We don't know how much of the
difference is biological because we have insisted girls be
one way and boys another. Are differences developed or are
they biological?

We can see examples of children's potential which has
been influenced by early training (or the lack of it.) I once
conducted strategic planning sessions for a south Texas
county. One woman named Juanita told me of her early life.
She said she had never felt accepted because she was
Mexican-American (another example of the "Life is
Contest" pattern). She didn't say this angrily, just as a
statement of fact. I thought, yeah, I also know I haven't felt
accepted. She said that as a child many of her generation
(she was in her mid-fifties) were not taught Spanish because
it would exclude them from white Anglo society. In her
case, however, her parents were from Mexico and didn't
speak English. So she grew up knowing Spanish and taught
it to four of her five children. She said her son who didn't
learn Spanish as a child learned it later and now he speaks
Spanish like an Anglo. All of her children had a similar
biological potential for fluency in Spanish. However, when
her one son did not learn Spanish early, his capability was
limited.

This is similar to what happens to women in an unfa-
vorable environment. If we do not learn skills early, we may
lose some of our innate biological capability. What we
might have been able to do, we never achieve. This is particularly true of muscular type activities. Are women not as

~ ~

strong as men because they can't be or because they didn't learn to be at an early age? Do men run faster in marathons because they are biologically different, or because they have been given different training? Did you know that the speed of women in the Olympics is increasing at a rate faster than men and if the trend continues women will eventually run as fast as or faster than men?

Schools influence gender differences by how they counsel boys and girls. Writer Chris Clarke-Epstein said that when she was in school, the students were given aptitude tests, but that the lists of professions considered suitable for girls and boys were completely different.

Because of the society we are raised in we will never know if women and men are biologically different. Important for us to decide, however, is that we can do whatever we choose, and our gender will not prevent us.

Men Are the Norm, Women the Exceptions

The assumption that men are the norm causes us problems. In the "Life is Contest" pattern, the experiences of the dominant group are heard, but the experiences of the dominated are not. For example, one reporter asked country music singer-composer Mary Chapin Carpenter if her songs were only for women because they were written from the female perspective. Why don't men need to hear the perspective and experiences of women too? Women hear the perspective and experiences of men from Garth Brooks and other male singers. The fact that the reporter could ask that question suggests that female singer-composers are a minority and that the dominant voice of country music comes from the male viewpoint. The pictures in our minds create our reality. As long as they dominantly profile men,

~ ~

we will continue to see more males in positions of authority — and more women in supporting roles.

One example of men being considered the norm in our society can be found in advertising. I've heard it said that the guideline for the ratio of males to females in advertising commercials is two to one. Ad agencies report that if more females appear in the ads, observers report that the ad was dominated by females.

As women enter previously male-only occupations, they often have heard such statements as "Women don't make good police officers," or "Women don't make good engineers." When the pioneering women succeeded in those areas, the response was "Well, they are the exception." Only when faced with many such successful pioneers does the idea begin to form that maybe women can do very well in occupations previously reserved for males.

We also have a responsibility to object when we see women treated as exceptions and not as full partners in the progress of our society.

Another result of the men-are-the-norm assumption is the annoyance and frustration of standing in line at public restrooms. Why do these long lines happen? Building codes specify the number of toilets in each restroom (based on the capacity of the building). Men's restrooms have the same number of toilets as women, and urinals in addition. It takes men 45 seconds on the average to use the restroom and women (with their different physiology) 79 seconds. All men have to do is zip and whip, and as you know, the process is much more involved for women. If women were considered to be the norm as much as men, a study would have been done long ago to arrive at the calculation that double the number of toilets for women in public restrooms should always be constructed.

Men Are More Valuable than Women

Studies show that men *and* women believe that men are more valuable than women. Harriet Lerner, author of *The Dance of Anger* says: "Being at the bottom of the seesaw relationship is culturally prescribed for women."[45]

This belief manifests itself in many subtle ways, including the space women occupy and the time women talk in groups. Sitting in a group, women take up less personal space by holding their arms and legs close to their bodies. Men spread their arms and legs out. (Of course, that doesn't mean men are spacey.) Research has shown that on an airplane, a man sitting next to a woman will get the arm rest. Although folk myth would have us believe that women talk more than men, research confirms that in mixed gender settings the reverse is true. In business meetings, women take fewer turns than men, talk for less time each turn, are interrupted more often, and are disagreed with more.

I have observed numerous other examples that demonstrate discrimination. For instance, when I ask a small group in seminars to assign a person to write notes, it is most frequently a woman who gets the task even if the group is mostly male.

Perhaps developers of entertainment also believe women are less important. Several years ago, a theme park was built in San Antonio called Fiesta Texas. It is a delightful experience, showcasing the many varied cultures of Texas. On my first trip I was feeling proud to be a Texan. That is until I went to the laser show at the end and found out that, as a woman, I wasn't a Texan after all. The laser show recaps the history of Texas in a breathtaking display of laser lights and fireworks. Hundreds of images of men flash on the limestone cliff: cowboys, stagecoach drivers,

~ ~

soldiers at the Alamo, farmers, politicians, musicians. Only a few women appeared out of the many images: a mother, two dancers and a handful of beautiful women as a backdrop to the song "Pretty Woman." The show leaves the impression that while men built Texas, women were nowhere to be seen. The final statement of the show sums it up: "Texans will always be cowboys."

Try to think of what women did in history. It's difficult, isn't it? Well, where were they? Biologically, we know that all those men represented in the Fiesta Texas laser show had to have mothers. Still, history largely ignores the contribution of women. They are invisible. Since women make up 51% of humanity, it makes statistical sense that one half or so of the images in the laser show should have been women.

Although we don't have a gender neutral word to describe male and female "cowboys" (cowgirl somehow just doesn't have the same connotation), I grew up with one in my family. My Aunt V was a rancher, married to a math teacher. She raised cattle, kept horses, killed rattlesnakes and kept javelinas as pets. With soft gray hair framing her crinkly face, Aunt V was no cowboy, but she did her share of roping, branding and herding. She would put a food pellet between her teeth and let her cows take it from her mouth. She did as she pleased, not what a woman was "supposed" to do. Aunt V was not the exception. There were many women ranchers, "cowgirls," in Texas.

Women made many other contributions to the development of the state of Texas. Women farmed, owned businesses, repaired covered wagons, and set up homesteads. Many were married, and many were heads of households. It is a woman-owned, Texas-based business that employs more women who are paid more than $50,000 annually than any other U. S. corporation: Mary Kay Cosmetics.

~ ~

Immortalized in the popular song, "Yellow Rose of Texas," although not in the Fiesta Texas light show, Emily Morgan was a black indentured servant. She went with Santa Anna, the attacker of the Alamo, to San Jacinto after the fall of the Alamo. Managing to get word to Sam Houston about Santa Anna's location, her efforts helped defeat the Mexican general and win the Texas Revolution.

Women have contributed to the economic health of the state. From ranches to boot manufacturing to literally building bridges, women have been at the forefront. Henrietta King (1832-1906) was the sole owner for 40 years of the King Ranch, the largest ranch in Texas. The Nacoma Boot Company, one of top three boot companies in the world, was founded and managed by Emid Justin. She is the world's only woman boot maker. Dallas owes its beginnings to a visionary business woman, Sarah Cochrell (1819-1892), who built the first iron bridge across Trinity River in 1872. She owned most of the Dallas Business District.

Texas women have contributed brilliantly to accomplishments in such diverse areas as sports, and aviation. Babe Didrikson Zaharias (1914-1956) won more gold medals and set more records in more sports than any other athlete, male or female, in the twentieth century. She said, "You've go to loosen your girdles, and really let the ball have it." Katherine Stinson (1891-1977) has been called the world's greatest woman pilot. She made her solo flight in 1912, 11years before Lindberg started flying.

Texas women are renowned in politics. Barbara Jordan, who later served three terms in the U. S. Congress, was the first black elected to the Texas Senate since Reconstruction. Judge Elma Salinas Ender was the first Mexican-American District Judge in the State of Texas. She endorses measures to prevent children from encountering legal problems, and seeks out opportunities to advocate equal opportunities for women in all arenas. Even Carrie Nation lived in Texas for 10 years.

Women have been active in preserving the rich history of the state of Texas. The buildings of the Alamo were saved by women. Adina Zavala and the D.R.T. (Daughters of Republic of Texas) convinced Clara Driscoll to contribute $25,000 and saved the Alamo from destruction. She also bought land surrounding the Alamo. Emily Edwards and the San Antonio Conservation Society in 1924 staged a puppet show to persuade the city commissioner to drop plans to pave over the San Antonio river as a flood control project.

Many popular women entertainers hail from Texas. All these women are Texans: Ginger Rogers, Sandy Duncan, Mary Martin, Cyd Charisse, Carol Burnett, Janis Joplin, Sissy Spacek, Farah Fawcett, Ester Phillips, Teresa Graves.

As women, we owe a debt of gratitude to the progress created by those pioneering women, some as ordinary as my Aunt V, who challenged limited thinking and pursued their dreams despite public opinion.

Being ignored and invisible in our society will continue to cause problems for women in acceptance in the business world. When we fail to visualize women in bold and notable historical situations, it is difficult to see them in bold and notable present-day situations making a difference in the world.

Women Are the Weaker Sex

Another accepted assumption is the old saw that women are the weaker sex. If women are the weaker sex, then why do we clean the toilets? If women are the weaker sex, then why do we have to pretend to be weaker, so as not

~ ~

to offend the men by our strength? Why do men need weak women to prove they are strong?

Harriet Lerner, author of *The Dance of Anger,* put it this way: "The weaker sex must protect the stronger sex from recognizing the strength of the weaker sex lest the stronger sex feel weakened by the strength of the weaker sex."[46]

Women pretend that men are stronger. Something about that seems dumb. The typical thinking goes like this:

Man: "I want to be stronger and smarter."

Woman: "Okay, I'll pretend you are — and I'll never let you see what I'm really like."

Man: "Okay, I'll pretend like I don't know you're pretending."

With all this pretending going on, where is there room for us, both women and men, to live as authentic human beings? Men have to go around being afraid of being found out that they are not as much as they've been pretending. Women have to go around being afraid they will show too much strength and they will be unlovable.

A friend of mine confessed that she pretended to be a little dumb and helpless to meet her husband. "I am embarrassed to say that how I met my husband was to go up to him and say 'Did you take good notes? I am a little confused on this subject, could you help me with it?'"

In my own case, when Peter and I were in college before we were married, we took a Fortran course together. We were in love already and sat next to each other in class. On the first test, I made a 95 and Peter made a 45. Guess who dropped the course? Me. I thought that he flunked because he was under so much pressure to do better than me. Later in the course, Peter was still doing poorly and he dropped the course. This is a good example of not

~ ~

competing with men, and of dimming our brightness lest it outshines theirs.

Women Are More Emotional than Men

Women are often accused of being more emotional, and often the myth of PMS is used to explain women's greater emotionality. In actuality, men's hormone levels are normally most similar to women's hormone levels during the pre-menstrual days.

It is true that our society grants more permission to women than to men to feel their emotions. Feeling your emotions is healthier physically and emotionally. Many experts believe that denying your emotions results in all kinds of illness, from heart attacks to ulcers to depression.

Rather than men and women being so different when it comes to emotions, it may be that in a couple, one person takes on the responsibility of expressing the emotions. Lerner describes it like this: "The more the man avoids sharing his own weaknesses, neediness, and vulnerability, the more his woman may experience and express more than her share."[47] Thus, the woman assumes the "job" of expressing the emotions for the couple.

Women Should Not Be Angry

I can't help but be amused by this assumption which would make of women placid angels who demonstrate enduring patience. Of course, women are angry. They want partnership status. Also, men should try walking around in heels and pantyhose for a day and see if they're not angry, too.

Seriously, women do suppress a lot of anger. The anger

results from being considered less valuable, less important, and as a result, their perception is ignored. When a woman's perception is not acknowledged, anger builds. The outcome is a well of anger among women that comes from domination. Anyone who is dominated experiences anger, whether it is the wife dominated by her husband, the husband dominated by his boss, or a friend dominated by another friend.

David Aronson, writer and editor of *Teaching Tolerance* magazine, observed,

> I think those who are tolerant and well meaning have to realize that there is an enormous well of anger that must be expressed before the tolerance can become reciprocal. And that makes people from the dominant group wary and impatient.... We have to recognize that there needs to be a period of healing. What happens next is that the side that has been making the rules, defining the history, explaining conquered people to themselves in language that is not their own, just has got to shut up and listen.[48]

Once, with a female friend, I allowed her needs to take precedence over mine in all of our interactions. I gave away my power, and allowed her to dominate. I bought into the power scheme. Eventually, I felt anger just the same.

Anger serves a valuable purpose for us. In *The Dance of Anger,* Lerner explained that we should value anger. "Anger is a signal, and one worth listening to. Our anger may be a message that we are being hurt, that our rights are being violated, that our needs or wants are not being adequately met, or simply that something is not right."[49]

Staying angry, however, keeps you in the same power structure you're trying to escape. You are still the dominated when you are angry. But, as Aronson said, you have to go through the anger to get to a point of healing. Why did I give my friend power over me? The answer is that I wanted to be validated by someone I respected. The problem was, when the illusion of her superiority vanished, she was no better than I or anyone else. She was merely an imperfect person just like everyone else. When I realized that, I was mad that I allowed myself to be tricked.

As a woman, I need to validate myself and give validity to my own experience and treasure that experience for what it is. If you value yourself for your uniqueness, then you are not so concerned that you are not fitting in. One experience you must validate for yourself is anger.

A final observation on the anger assumption is actually a corollary to the "Women shouldn't be angry" idea. That is, "If you are angry, you are a bitch."

To make changes, we may have to challenge the norms of the group or of society. Normally roses are not thrown at our feet when we do that. Usually we are told to get back in line. This is a phenomenon which happens to women when they are called "bitch." Actually, the bitch accusation is a weapon used by one person to control another. If you step out of the "feminine" stereotype, chances are you will be called a bitch.

Lerner makes an interesting observation about name-calling: "It is an interesting sidelight that our language — created and codified by men — does not have *one* unflattering term to describe men who vent their anger at women."[50]

I believe that if you haven't been called "bitch" yet, you aren't trying hard enough.

Keep in mind that women are not the only ones who are told to get back in line. A man named Wes was in a strategic planning session I conducted. He told me that in high school his teacher asked the boys: "How many of you like *Pride and Prejudice?*" Wes raised his hand. None of the other boys did. The teacher said, "That's funny I never had a boy who liked *Pride and Prejudice* before." Wes wanted to crawl into a hole.

Women Must Be Less Successful Than Men

Here's a major assumption which has burdened women enormously. Women shouldn't be too successful.

One day I read this quotation in a newspaper: "Failure unsexes a man, success unsexes a woman." Is this a limiting assumption or what? What do failure and success have to do with gender?

First, failure and success are relative. You can't fail if you are discovering. You may know an action didn't work for you but you haven't failed. As for success unsexing a woman, this statement carries the hidden message that the price a woman must pay for her success is the "loss of gender identification."

It's easy to become incensed at the outrageousness of myths such as this projected onto the female (and male) sex. Women know that success has nothing to do with sex. The only way a female or male can be unsexed is surgically. We know that all human beings are born wanting to achieve. If we weren't, we wouldn't learn to walk. But little girls are taught early not to try to achieve too hard or no one will love them.

Because of this early training and the "Life is Contest" pattern, women have become externally focused and have looked to others for approval. We need to listen to our internal voices and follow our own maps. We also have to

~ ~

trust that, when we are our own authentic (and successful) selves, there will be those men who will appreciate us and who will be available to share our love. There are many men who would love to love a successful woman. My definition of a man as a failure is one who cannot love a successful woman.

Squandering your potential to avoid being "unsexed" is a poor bargain. Avoiding failure (which limits your success) is a poor bargain also.

Sometimes the "women must be less successful" assumption takes the form of "men are -smarter than women." When the developers of the Stanford-Benet Intelligence test were field testing their landmark instrument, they found that women consistently scored higher than men. The developers assumed that men were smarter than women and therefore the test must be defective. So they went back and rewrote the test so that men could score as high as women. If the situation had been reversed and men had tested higher than women, can't you just see the headlines now: "Intelligence test proves men are smarter than women."

The Woman's Career Is Secondary to the Man's

In the past, most people assumed that women would stay home and keep house. When women entered the work force, most people assumed their work was to supplement the husband's income. Obviously, these assumptions placed women in an inferior support role in which their own dreams of achievement were secondary.

Chris Clarke-Epstein grew up believing that she would have a family and a career. Although she was a straight-A math and science student, she was counseled to be an

English teacher. She went to college to be a teacher. Before she finished college, she fell in love, got pregnant and married. Although she had maintained her straight-A grades in college, and her husband was a mediocre student, her husband stayed in school and there was no discussion about the subject. Chris dropped out and went to work as a waitress to support their new family. They silently assumed that Chris's career would be secondary to her husband's.

Another woman told me she majored in child and family development. She wanted to open a chain of day-care centers. After college, she went to work for K-Mart as an assistant store manager. She and her husband decided that her career would take a back seat to his and she dropped out of the training program that would have qualified her for promotions. She trained others who were promoted above her because she had removed herself from the management track. The couple moved to Houston where he worked as a landscape architect. Two years later, the bottom fell out of the building market and her husband experienced tough times in his field.

In this day of insecure employment, frequent recessions and high divorce rate, it is not smart for a family to put all its financial eggs in the husband's career basket. Strategically, it is not smart for women to agree to an arrangement in which she puts off her career development.

Statistics indicate that the likelihood of divorce is very real. If the woman has subordinated her career to the husband's, then her standard of living will be inferior in the case of a divorce. National statistics show that this is the case. They indicate plainly that after divorce a woman's standard of living declines, while the man's actually increases. The majority of families whose standard of living falls below the poverty level are those headed by women.

~ ~

Men Should Wear the Pants In the Family

For the reasons discussed above and because wasted intelligence is economic loss, the male as the undisputed authority in a family is a faulty assumption. Actually this assumption has several levels of meaning. One is that we should accept the authority of the man no matter how much or how little he knows. This assumption insists that women turn off their brains, refuse to consider who is best qualified to make a specific decision and defer to the male, solely because he is a male.

Perhaps we have moved beyond the apparent stupidity of this assumption, but this kind of belief still has a strong echo in our society and undermines women's efforts to assert themselves. Women dominating men is no better than men dominating women. However, a woman does not have to be very dominating to be accused of wearing the pants in her family. This statement is used to insult a woman and manipulate her into more "ladylike" (read stereotypical) behavior.

This slur also negatively affects relationships in situations where the woman's salary exceeds her husband's. The "Life is Contest" pattern reinforces the belief that men must earn more than their wives or risk challenge to their masculinity. In a more sensible "Life is Connection" situation, there would be no upset of equilibrium if the woman made more than the man in a marriage situation.

Women Must Be the Primary Caretakers

"Now, as always, the most automated appliance in a household is the mother."

— *Beverly Jones*

Does it make sense to base division of labor within a family on gender rather than talents and desires?

The mother of a marketing professor I know got a degree in economics from an ivy-league college. She couldn't find work so she went to work in a typing pool.

One day she typed an ad for a job and she said, "I could do this job." She went to the person hiring and said "I want this job." He said, "No, you have to have a degree." She said "I have a degree." He said, "No, you have to have a degree from an ivy league college." She said, "I have a degree from an ivy league college." He said, "No. You have to have a degree in economics." She said, "I have a degree in economics." She got the job. She worked at that job until she had children and then she quit to stay home.

When her children (a boy and a girl two years apart) were in school, she went back to college and got a teaching degree and taught first grade the rest of her professional life. She was miserable at it. Why didn't she go back to a career in economics? The answer to that must be the expectation family and society have that women should be available for their children. This unconscious, but pervasive, pressure may have led to her choice of teaching. Her husband was more laid back and not driven to achieve. But she, as demonstrated by her early life, was a go-getter and an achiever. Both the man and the woman in this case made choices that didn't fit them, but were in keeping with the prescribed behavior by gender.

What a waste! When we try to fit our lives into the sex stereotypes rather than looking at our innate talents and strengths, we all suffer. Here was a woman of drive, intelligence and ambition. Her mate was not particularly motivated to achieve and didn't desire an ambitious career. He was an adequate provider for the family. However, he

~ ~

might have been happier (given a world that made room for differences among males) to have stayed home and taken care of the kids. His more ambitious wife might have been happier pursuing the primary career.

A corollary to the women-must-be-the-primary-care-takers assumption is that "women's work" is not important work. Madonna Kolbenschlag, author of *Kiss Sleeping Beauty Good-bye,* observed that "Women were relegated to an inferior caste ... most dramatically with the coming of industrialization. 'Women's work' was segregated from significant human activity."[51]

Isn't it interesting that among traditional women's choices, the care of future generations was considered to be insignificant? Those insignificant activities, marriage and family, certainly have added extra challenges to building the life you wish to build.

Women Can [Can't] Have It All

This assumption is based on the belief that maintaining the household "belongs" to the woman, and that the woman's family duties take priority over her professional achievement. This assumption makes the unfair assessment that women can have professional success or relationship success but not both.

No one seems to ask the question of whether men can have it all. The limitation is applied only to women. An interesting study emerged which discussed that among top executives, 90 percent of males had children. Only 35 percent of the females had children. Why? Because 100 percent of the male executives with children had wives. As males, they weren't expected to have it all!

From my experience, I think it's safe to say that most women would prefer not to have it all. We'd like to give away the laundry, dishes, and toilet cleaning. We'll keep the fun stuff — like exercising our creative talents and cuddling with the kids. As Heloise said, "I think housework is the reason most women go to the office."

Housework Is Women's Work

"[Women] can go wherever they want — as long as we teach men how to do housework! The world will really change for us when they start doing their share."

— Sally Jessy Raphael

While the assumption that housework is women's work is being challenged by couples who do cooperate with household chores, in the main women are still considered the principal homemakers. In order for women to pursue their goals, family and home must become the responsibility of all involved. As long as family and home are only women's responsibility, the time and energy necessary for the wife to pursue her dreams will be rationed.

Sociologist Arlie Hochschild, author of *The Second Shift*, studied ten two-career couples over a twelve year period. She found that women did 75% of the housework, including such traditionally masculine tasks as yard work and car care. In fact, women labored at home fifteen hours per week more than men. Over a year's time this extra labor adds up to an extra *month* of twenty-four-hour days. Men, with all that extra time, on the average sleep one-half hour more per day and watch an extra hour of television per day.

Hochschild did not notice any movement toward men and women sharing the household chores more equitably over the 12 years of her study (1976-1988). Interestingly, however, while the spouses didn't share the work any more equally, after the study they imagined (and reported) that they did. One couple, after fighting over the sharing for a period of years, finally reported that they had divided the housework equally. They settled on the solution that the wife would take responsibility for the upstairs and the husband would take the downstairs. Sounds fair, right? Unfortunately, the upstairs included the bedrooms, the bathrooms, the kitchen and the laundry. The downstairs included the garage and the yard.

Hochschild found that the men who said they were helping the most in fact helped the least.

For women to have the energy to pursue their dreams, both the ownership and the completion of the housework must begin to be shared equally by both genders.

John Gray, author of *Men Are from Mars, Women Are from Venus,* describes in his book how he "helps" his wife by going to get milk. He is pleased and rewarded when his wife brags about his "help." Soon, he reported, he was looking forward to getting milk *for her.*

What's wrong with this picture?

Doesn't Gray drink milk? Why doesn't he take responsibility for the milk himself, rather than doing it *for her?*

When my husband, Peter, and I first discussed marriage, I told him that I would not get married if it meant I had to do all of the housework.

"No problem," Peter agreed. "We'll share the housework fifty-fifty."

We got married and began to share. Probably, ten years later, Peter told me one evening, as he had often before, "I loaded the dishwasher for you."

That day it hit me like a ton of bricks. He loaded it for me? He hadn't used any dishes? Although we had been sharing the duties, the ownership of the housework was still mine in both his head and mine. When Peter did housework, he was proud because he was "helping" me. When I did housework, no one (including me) noticed or commented.

A recent "Phil Donahue" show[52] hosted a segment on men who did not "help" their wives with the housework. A professor/expert on his show brought up the point that there are two shifts of work. This is the concept that Hochschild outlined in her book. The professor/expert said that we must think in terms of a day shift and an evening shift. The partners in a marriage need to share in both. Her best point was that we should move beyond men thinking they are helping with the housework to a frame of mind that clearly understands the idea of sharing chores.

The wives on the Donahue show said that their husbands asked them to fetch and carry — drinks, the TV remote control, snacks and other things. The wives complied. Serving your mate is fine if it's reciprocal between husband and wife. Resentment arises when fetch and carry is one-sided.

One of the funniest things I heard from the show was the revelation of a woman whose husband threw his underwear on the floor, he expected her to pick it up and wash it. She nailed it to the floor.

Women Must Be Beautiful

When a woman I know was in high school, a woman's organization held an essay contest. Contestants were asked to write about the future. She won the contest and the paper ran the pictures of the winners. The headline said "Beauties with Brains." She said she was glad the editors put the word "beauties" in the headline because, although she was pleased to be smart, she was more interested in getting a date Saturday night.

When women are judged on beauty, they are praised for their looks rather than for their accomplishments. All of us can take steps to pursue accomplishment, but we have limited effect on our looks. Also the hours and money we spend to look better according to media standards have limited returns in terms of enjoyment or success.

What Can You Do about the Assumptions that Hinder Women's Success?

I've listed and examined several common assumptions by which women are judged and which overlay much social behavior. But how do we remove these restrictions on women's freedom?

First, merely becoming aware of the assumptions helps us overcome them. One example of corrective action might be that of personally addressing the idea that women talk more than men. As I mentioned, research has shown that men talk more than women in mixed gender meetings. When you think you may be speaking out too much in a group, you can test yourself with the question: "Am I speaking more than the others, or am I speaking more than my picture of how much women should talk?"

Another method to dismantle erroneous assumptions is through teaching ourselves and our children that women and men behave in many, many different ways. Whether or not an individual of either sex matches a traditional stereo-type, she or he is valuable, important, and has many contri-

~ ~

butions to make to our society. Any human trait or characteristic can have good or bad results. It depends on your actions. As a society we need to learn acceptance and tolerance for different ways of being. It's okay to be different. We are who and what we are.

A third way to combat discrimination against women is to encourage businesses to make certain that objective evaluations are used to advance and promote women. With women pouring into the work force in record numbers, and into many new opportunities, they still face unequal compensation and treatment, frequently because decisions are made based on subjective evaluations which are unconsciously biased. As a result, less than one percent of all working women make more than $50,000 and less than two percent of corporate officers in Fortune 500 companies are women.

It's old news, but women still average $.57 on the dollar compared to men. At executive levels, women earn $.43 for every dollar men make. Until our society has progressed to a much more egalitarian state, we need to make sure that opportunities are not prevented by subtle forms of discrimination. The only way to do that is to use objective measures of evaluation.

Gender-Biased Language

Another simple step that anyone can take to help reduce limiting assumptions is to stop using gender-biased language. Gender-biased language reinforces the men-are-the-norm assumption by leaving women out. Those who codified the English language decided that we didn't need words that were inclusive of men and women. Instead, key words would permit the masculine reference to indicate all

~ ~

of humanity. So, "man" came to stand for human (man and woman), and the masculine "he" could indicate either sex. However, "she" could not mean "he."

Using the noun "man" for both sexes is ambiguous and requires listeners or readers to translate in their heads. Often writers will say they use the masculine to represent gender-neutral because it is less cumbersome. What is less cumbersome about placing the burden on the reader (listener) of translating or figuring out exactly what the writer meant? What we need in English is a word that truly designates men and women, and he or she.

Here is another interesting flaw in the logic of gender-biased language. A writer is required by the rules to be precise about the singular/plural of a word usage and pronoun agreement, rather than to be precise about the gender. This means that if you write the statement, "A consultant divides *his* time between marketing and consulting," the gender may be inaccurate because the consultant could be a woman. If you write the statement, "A consultant divides *their* time between marketing and consulting," the gender is more accurately non-specific, but you have erred according to the grammar rules. Who made up those rules, anyway?

Language perpetuates beliefs so subtly that we are not even aware that we are being taught the "right way" for things to be. Language is so pervasive and so unconscious that we stop questioning its appropriateness. Children notice. Children ask why do we use man to mean men and women? But soon enough we swallow the explanation — weak though it may be — that it's for okay man to mean men and women.

The result of gender-biased language is that men became the norm and women became the exception. By

~ ~

leaving women out of language, our society left women out of the thoughts of the people, since thoughts are conveyed by words. One research study demonstrated the results of this omission.

Research shows that masculine words used to represent both sexes do, in fact, cause women to be forgotten. When you learned about primitive man, what picture did you have in your mind? In one study, science students were given assignments describing and drawing their views of primitive humans. In this study, three groups were asked to draw pictures of primitive humans and the instructions used varying degrees of gender-biased language. The first group's instructions used the terms "man," "men," "mankind" and "he." The second group's instructions used the more neutral terms "humans," "people" and "they." The third group's instructions used the inclusive terms "men and women," and "they."

In the first two groups, both male and female students consistently drew only male figures. In the third group, significantly more female figures were drawn than in the first two groups. The fact that the students did not draw female images when the terms "man," "mankind," and "he" were used indicates that those terms do exclude females in our thinking.

Masculine words do not represent men and women despite what we have been taught. As the science student research showed, masculine words used to represent men and women cause women to be forgotten. The result of gender-biased language is to unconsciously reinforce and perpetuate sexism. By thinking and speaking with gender-biased language, we ignore and devalue women.

I recently read the following sentence in a business publication: "Businessmen are routinely frustrated by the

~ ~

public's shifting tastes."

Of course, we have been taught that the masculine word "businessmen" means both men and women. Unfortunately, women are, in fact, excluded by the term. Women are involved in businesses and women also try to match their products to the public's tastes. Ironically, the remainder of the article focused on women's fashions. Revising sentences shows sensitivity and receptivity to women in the business world. Some options: "Business decision-makers," "Product managers," "Retailers."

We talk the way we think, and we think the way we talk. Language is a pervasive and subtle reinforcer of our views of ourselves. Our language reflects women's roles in society, but our language also creates acceptable women's roles.

By thinking and speaking of men first and women as an afterthought, gender-biased language causes sexism which is so subtle that we do not recognize it. Using gender-biased language unconsciously reinforces and perpetuates limiting views for women.

To foster a better environment for women, we must avoid using masculine terms to represent men and women. Make it a practice to rewrite sentence structure so that gender content is neutral.

Chapter Seven
Development

~ ~

"Even if you're on the right track, you'll get run over if you just sit there."

— Will Rogers

Once you have set your goals, you may not know how to achieve many of them. That's okay. For now you begin the process of development, learning how to achieve those goals and objectives you have set for yourself.

Methods of learning are all around you, from formal university courses to informal across-the-back-fence talks with the neighbors. Whatever you have set your sights on, you can find out how to progress toward it by asking questions and by learning.

~ ~

Understand Power

"Power is America's last dirty word. It is easier to talk about money — and much easier to talk about sex — than it is to talk about power."[53]
— *Rosabeth Moss Kanter*

To accomplish your plan, you may need to develop power in areas critical to your success. The acquisition of personal power earned a bad reputation in recent years. Probably because of the "Life is Contest" pattern women have come to confuse power with being forced to do things against our will. Due to negative beliefs about power and women being powerful, women often avoid leadership positions which confer power.

Power, by itself, is neither good nor bad. The negative image of power is frequently the result of not having a true sense of your own power. That dominating kind of power is an attempt to cover up feelings of powerlessness. People who are confident of their power don't have to dominate.

Recently I discussed gender issues with the president of a company. He said, "I have to be honest with you. My first vice-president is overbearing, bossy and dominating. She doesn't need to be that way. I believe in listening and cooperating." I discovered that the woman vice-president held a position of power within the company, but she did not expect her power to be respected. To compensate for feeling out of control, and to attempt to be powerful, she commanded others. However, she was undermining her power by being domineering, therefore, making the situation all the worse.

~ ~

Kanter explains positive power:

Powerful managers have so many lines of connection and thus are oriented outward, they tend to let go of control downward, developing more independently functioning lieutenants. The powerless live in a different world. Lacking the supplies, information, or support to make things happen easily, they may turn instead to the ultimate weapon of those who lack productive power — oppressive power: holding others back and punishing with whatever threats they can muster.[54]

Being powerful is not negative for women. To accomplish our goals, we must have power. With power, we can act quickly to accomplish more. True power leads to shared power and cooperation. Power within a business organization results from access to resources and information.

Increasing your power within an organization can help you achieve more for your organization. At the same time, you can energize your progress toward your personal goals. To increase your power, look at the sources of power in your company. Power results from access to lines of supplies, information, and support.[55] Supplies include equipment required to accomplish your department's goals, and budgets to be able to move forward. Information is vital in today's information age. The better access to information you have, and the more effectively you can use that information, the more powerful you can become within your organization. Lines of support are crucial because no one can accomplish great things alone. Teamwork is an essential part of success in today's organizations.

~ ~

Expanding Personal Power

"Power can be seen as power with rather than
power over, and it can be used for competence and
cooperation, rather than dominance and control."
                                          — *Anne Barstow*

To expand your power look at your job position.
Powerful jobs have three characteristics: discretion, visibility, and relevance. Many traditional female positions
have not filled these necessary criteria.

Discretion. If your position allows you flexibility to
design new and creative solutions to your organization's
problems, you will have more opportunities to develop
power.

Visibility. Even if you design and implement brilliant
solutions, the increase of your power will be limited unless
others in your organization know about your accomplishments. You must be visible within the organization, and gain
recognition and notice.

Relevance. Your job must be seen by the organization
as relevant. Relevance means you are solving pressing organizational problems, such as improving profitability or
productivity. Without relevance your power will be limited.

To expand your professional power, you may have to
be willing to do things others are reluctant to do. Jill Griffin,
whom you met earlier, was once asked to speak at a plant.
Because of the times of the shift changes the assignment
required that she speak at five a.m. Jill enthusiastically took
over this unpleasant task for her brand manager. It turned
out to be a great opportunity for her. The plant manager was
not thrilled at the prospect of a young, female marketing
assistant being sent in as a replacement for the brand

manager. After hearing Jill handle the question and answer period, however, his attitude changed. He became a great ally to Jill, writing a letter to her department head and asking her to come back to speak to the plant often. When the plant manager was later promoted to the president of RJR, he was pivotal to Jill's promotion. Jill rocketed from marketing assistant to brand manager passing over six other brand managers with more experience than she had. Jill believes her willingness to give presentations gave her the edge.

Besides having a potentially powerful position you must have an effective support network to attain power. Far from the old practice of ruthlessly climbing over people on your way to the top you are much more likely to reach the top if you have mutually beneficial relationships. Your support network should include sponsors, peer networks, and subordinates. You need sponsors above you in the organization who will champion your causes and recommend you for opportunities. You need networks of your peers to share information and help you get access to supplies. You need subordinates whom you are helping to gain power themselves. Powerful people are seen as such because they have the capacity to give power to others and they do so.

Networking Your Way to Power

Networking helps you on your path to success. With networking you can get the information and the contacts you need to move forward with your plans. Participating in civic organizations or other professional organizations is a good way to become known and visible. When volunteering, take on only as much as you can accomplish to a top-quality level. Do your best because people watch the

~ ~

way you handle your volunteer activities and believe that is how you will handle any professional obligations. Whatever you agree to do, keep your commitments. Ask questions of everyone you meet to help flesh out your knowledge about your chosen goals. Get the information you need to develop your goals into reality.

How to Make Networking Work

Set networking goals. Decide what you need and write down specifically what you want as a goal. Do you want a better idea, more information or resources? What kind of ideas, information or resources do you need?

Match the type of networking to your goals. If you need more prospects for your business, a leads club is what you want. If you want to keep up to date in your profession, your professional organization is your best bet.

Prepare a 25-word introduction. State what you do in simple, easy to understand terms. Don't say "I am a lawyer." Say "I specialize in corporate takeover law for medium to large corporations. I show corporations how to retain their assets in case of a takeover."

Have a distinctive business card. Use color and a logo. Then, pass out as many as you can at every opportunity. The game is she who passes out her whole box of one thousand first wins.

Listen carefully. People appreciate a listener and are more likely to respond with the help you need.

Keep careful records. The more information you keep on everyone you meet, the better. Be sure to note the name of spouse, birthdays, personal likes and dislikes, and areas of knowledge. A simple index card file will do, but computer databases are much better.

~ ~

Send thank you notes. Set a goal to send five per day to your resources. Let people know you appreciate them both verbally and in written notes.

Share credit. Look for reasons to acknowledge others. If you can talk up someone else for any reason, do it. The next thing you know, she will be talking you up.

Strive for quality. If you do not have time to do an excellent volunteer job, say no. Say yes to those projects that match your goals and permit you to show people what excellent work you do.

Help others and ask for help. Consciously look for opportunities to help others and don't be afraid to ask for the assistance you need. You will get it!

Power Plays

Much discrimination in business today is so subtle that we have a lot of trouble recognizing it. I had lunch with a businessman (old enough to be my father). A very successful and well-connected man, he was retired and starting a new business. He said several times how beautiful a woman I was and made several jokes about him having lunch with "another woman" (other than his wife). He touched me several times "warmly" on the hands and kissed me on greeting and leaving. Because we were merely acquaintances and not old friends, I felt very uncomfortable with all that but it is very hard to be upset with someone who is so friendly and so "affectionate." Even so, I felt like I was being told in no uncertain terms that I was the subordinate and he was the one with power.

How many other instances are there every day of such subtle put-downs? How many such subtle put-downs have we endured from our friends and lovers? Even worse, we frequently don't notice it. We think they are right that we are worth less because of our femaleness which translates to "worthlessness." Our friends and lovers are not aware of it either. In relationships, we need to pay attention to times when we feel unexplainably distressed. We may discover that the relationship is better for them than for us.

Recognizing Our Power

"Unfortunately, there are still many women in the business world who refuse to support women. I call them 'Honorary Males' — women who think that power is to be had only in the company of men. Women must realize they have power — economic and political. Don't give your power away; use it for yourself and for the benefit of other women."

— *Ginger Purdy*

As women, we often have power that we do not recognize ourselves. For instance, women represent the power of decision on millions of dollars of purchases. Companies even now are realizing that women represent a huge market that they must court or they will lose sales.

As women become more integrated into the idea and practice of power the following incident will occur less often:

Linda Coffey, a dermatologist, was investigating the purchase of computer equipment. She shared office space and staff with a male dermatologist. She did all the pre-purchase legwork and research on a suitable computer system. When the salesperson (a man) presented his computer equipment to her and her male colleague, it was her colleague the salesman invited to play golf. Linda was

~ ~

furious to have been ignored and at the salesman's assumption that the male colleague would make the buying decision. Linda exercised her power and blocked the order.

As more women recognize that their purchasing decisions constitute power, salespeople and companies will also begin to realize the power of women.

Asking for What You Want

"A child of one can be taught not to do certain things such as touch a hot stove, turn on the gas, pull lamps off tables by their cords, or wake mommy before noon."

— *Joan Rivers*

One skill that you must learn if you are to live your own true life is to ask for what you want. This is not what you were taught. Women tend to put their own needs and wishes last — right after their spouses, lovers, children and friends. Is it any wonder that we feel so empty and are not nourished?

Asking for what you want takes a lot of courage — because it isn't socially acceptable. "You are selfish," you are told. "Don't you even care about your children?" Of course you care about your children. As a rule, the accusation stops you dead in your tracks, and you can't think of a way to answer. It is small comfort to you to hear that yes, you must take care of yourself before you can take care of others. You hear, but you do not believe.

This is an example of falling into believing the pattern of "Life is Contest." The pattern leads you to believe that there can be only one winner, and its either you or them. Remind yourself that another option is "Life is

Connection," and that you must be connected with yourself first before you can develop healthy connections with others. Look for ways to ask for what you want that lead to connection between your true self and your significant others.

Help them to understand what they can do to help. Sometimes the assistance we need is just to have the space to do it. Other times, we need the family to cooperate and do their chores so that we can spend time on our dreams. Let them know that they are helping you work on your dreams by being cooperative.

Show your family your progress on a chart. Remind them in an appeal for cooperation that, "Just fifteen minutes of silence would help me make three more phone calls to get information for my goal."

Build in rewards consistent with their efforts. If you are trying to read a book and you have a two-year-old who wants you to play, perhaps you can set up an exchange bargain: 15 minutes of quiet play while you read for 15 minutes of mother's attention. When my children were young, I used this technique frequently. It took longer this way for me to accomplish my objectives, but I could combine business with the reward of raising happy, healthy kids.

As the kids grow older, you can offer to pay them for doing activities. My children make handouts, file, enter names in my database and I pay them for their efforts.

Other ideas for rewards include: a trip to the movies or to the mall, a visit to the zoo or museum, a new book, an ice cream sundae, a day off from doing the dishes, 30 minutes later bedtime, 30 minutes extra TV, a friend over to spend the night on the weekend, a long distance phone call to a friend who has moved away, 15 minutes of playing a game, collecting chips or beans that can later be exchanged for a prize or toy, a sticker, or a star on a chart.

Guilt

"The only thing that seems eternal and natural in motherhood is ambivalence."
— Jane Lazarre

The biggest occupational hazard we face as women trying to combine our dreams, careers, and relationships is guilt. When we are at work we are guilty that we are not with our children. When we are with our children we are guilty about the report sitting on our desk. When we are at home we are guilty about the dust bunnies growing into dust bears in every corner of every room. What do we do about this guilt?

First, get factual information. If you feel guilty about your children being in day care, research the subject. Studies show that children in day care do equally as well as children who stay at home. In fact there are benefits to day care including improved social skills. Whatever your pet guilt trip is, make sure you know the facts.

Second, your goals help you separate the important from the merely urgent activities. Plan time every day for the important things in your life. Dust bunnies may seem urgent, but they will wait. The bedtime story for your growing children will not wait. They will be grown soon.

Third, refuse to allow yourself to feel guilty. Decide how much time you will spend with the kids, how much at work. You can always adjust this decision in times of need. If the child is sick, more time will be needed this week. If a crisis happens at work, work will get more time this week.

~ ~

If both happen at once, do the best you can, but leave the guilt behind. You just don't have time for it!

Jane Tait advises, "Don't let the guilt get to you." That's how she deals with her critical inner voice and the guilt. She also says don't lose your humor. The kids do grow up. There is a life. It does get better.

Of course, all of us have to struggle with guilt and the negative reinforcement we get when we choose to resist the expectations of others. All my married life I have been teased that I have my husband well trained. Imagine reversing that. Would anyone ever accuse a husband of having his wife well trained?

Actually, women are already well trained by the time we get married and that training seldom fashions us to pursue objectives that make sense for us personally. As a rule we are molded to fit into a gender role prescribed for us. Peter, my husband, likes to drive the kids to their various activities. I don't particularly like driving around town. So he does most of the driving. I feel guilty because I think if I were a really good mother, I would want to do the driving. What I object to is the time driving takes out of work schedules. I love the kids and I love to spend time with them. But frankly the driving is not my favorite sport. If Peter doesn't mind, it makes sense for him to do the driving and I can do other things which I prefer.

Personal preferences and role expectations are balances all of us have to work out. Part of what gets in our way is the "shoulds." Real women do this, real men do that (and never the twain shall meet). Examine the shoulds in your life and make certain they make sense in terms of your important objectives.

Chapter Eight
Risk and Conflict

~ ~

Take Risks

"Every time you meet a situation, though you think at the time it is an impossibility and you go through the torture of the damned, once you have met it and lived through it, you find that forever after you are freer than you were before."

— *Eleanor Roosevelt*

Success demands risk. Before starting my business, I needed information on what kind of business to start and how to get started. I wanted to ask several people about their experiences to find out what I needed to do to begin my business. At the time, it seemed like a huge risk to me to call someone up on the telephone and to ask her or him to help me in some way. I don't know why the idea of asking for help intimidated me, but it did. I was afraid they would not

~ ~

want to help me. Perhaps they would be rude to me or perhaps I would seem bothersome to them. It took all the guts I had to dial the numbers, praying all the while that they wouldn't be there. When luckily my prayers were not answered, and I reached my contacts, their reaction was completely different than the reaction I feared. All of the people I called were enthusiastic about helping me — and *were flattered* that I had called them. Was I ever surprised, relieved and delighted! Now I no longer fear making that type of call.

Whatever your stage in life may be there may be something you need to do that involves risk. It may be as simple as making a telephone call or speaking to a group. It may be that doing what frightens you is the risk which will build your confidence, and lead to your success.

Push Yourself Out of Your Envelope

"You will do foolish things, but do them with enthusiasm."

— *Collette*

Push yourself out of your envelope. One of my favorite quotes is, "If your palms aren't sweating, you aren't in the game." If you are to grow, you must venture into unknown territory. Unknown territory is scary. Do something you are afraid to do every day. Fear keeps us from taking the steps we need to take to achieve success. How often have you made excuses to yourself like these? "But I don't have enough money." "I don't have enough time." "They might get mad." "I don't know enough."

While waiting for the shuttle bus to take me to the airport, I met a nurse who had been at the Dermatological

Nurses Association convention. Speaking with a soft country West Texas accent, she told me she was from Amarillo, although she grew up in Montana. She sure had picked up the Amarillo way of speaking. I asked her where her suitcase was. She said she had flown only twice and was scared of getting lost and missing connections. Because of her fear, for a three-day stay she had brought only one small carry-on bag. I was amazed. I had my carry-on backpack, my museum-size Samsonite, and my wheeled carry-on bag. Flying was a risk for the nurse, but I bet the next time she flies she will be more comfortable.

Thinking about the nurse led me to reflect on my first ever sales call. Fear comes in different forms and I remember finding it hard to breathe for two hours before that first tentative meeting with a prospect. During the meeting, I felt my neck getting redder and redder. When I left, I looked in the rear view mirror and realized how red I was. I was embarrassed. I wondered what the prospect thought about my flustered complexion. Did she think I had turned red because I didn't really know what I was talking about? I wasn't really sure myself if I knew what I was talking about. I had felt terribly stressed by my self-generated urgency to get that person to buy from me. Of course, since that stumbling first call, I have taken sales courses to make sure I am presenting myself in the best possible way. The pressure I put on myself is now gone and I actually have fun on sales calls.

A flustered feeling is common to many who stretch themselves beyond previous boundaries. At first it is hard, but I promise, it does get easier. The journey to success takes practice. As you practice, you get better. We forget the lesson of risk that we learned growing up. It takes lots of risks to become an adult, and the rewards are great. Often,

~ ~

though, maturity operates like a caution brake and we avoid risks.

At the zoo, I saw a man in his twenties buy a bag of blue cotton candy. He had a little girl, I guess his daughter, with him. She looked at the cotton candy and said incredulously, "You aren't going to eat that are you?" The father said, "I thought I would. Don't you want some?"

She shook her head as vigorously as a washing machine agitator on power wash. Nonchalantly, the father opened the bag and took out a wad of cotton candy. The little girl jumped back as if the cotton candy would sting her. So he took a bite while the little girl watched with eyes as wide as the Gulf of Mexico. He held it out for her for her to take. She put her hands behind her back. She leaned over and licked the candy. Then she licked it again. Then she took the piece out of his hand and began to eat with relish. Had the little girl not taken the risk, she would have never learned what great stuff cotton candy is.

The Opposite Tack

To move forward we all have to learn. To learn we have to be willing to make mistakes. Be flexible enough to change your approach if it is not working. One definition of insanity is doing the same thing repeatedly and expecting different results. If what you are doing is not producing the results you want, try something different. I call it the "Opposite Tack." Very frequently, our instincts prevent us from taking the action we need to achieve what we want. Do the opposite of what you normally would do.

One example is resisting your children. Maybe your son or daughter comes in and says, "You never take me seriously." Don't give them the usual response: "Of course

~ ~

I take you seriously. Remember just last week when you ..." Say: "You could be right. That's going to change starting now. What do you want me to hear?" Then listen very carefully.

I found another example of the Opposite Tack once when I made a suggestion to my daughter and she rolled her eyes. Usually, I don't enjoy her rolling her eyes. I receive the message as a put-down, meaning something roughly like, "What a stupid mother, not to mention human being, you are. I am frankly amazed you haven't been put out of your misery long ago." I really want her to quit rolling her eyes, but I have never succeeded by commanding her to quit. This time I said to her, "My goal is to get you to roll your eyes five times every day." She and I both burst out laughing, and it was a long time before she rolled her eyes again.

Taking the Opposite Tack could take the form of doing something you normally would avoid. For example, if you find yourself in a business situation you can't change, but you know others are not happy, your normal reaction might be to pretend everything is okay and forge ahead. Try the Opposite Tack and instead put your cards on the table.

Once I conducted a Saturday seminar for a group of 80 employees who were not at all happy about being asked to come in on a Saturday. At the beginning of the seminar, I noticed the closed body language of the participants. To put it mildly, they were not happy. I knew for them to get anything out of the session they would have to get over this conflict. Normally, I would have just ignored those feelings and kept going, enduring the discomfort while hoping that somehow the unstated would evaporate.

This time, I decided to try the Opposite Tack. So I asked, "How many of you did not want to come today?"

~ ~

There was a little embarrassed tittering and most of the hands went up. I continued: "Take a good look at those who didn't want to be here and be sure to give them a little extra appreciation for coming even though they didn't want to." Then I asked, "How many of you wanted to come today?" A few hands went up. I continued: "Notice who they are and give them appreciation for being here because they came and they wanted to come."

The tension dissolved, the group settled down to the material and the session turned out to be very successful. Just acknowledging the group's feelings, though some were negative, was enough to get the group moving in the desired direction. Doing the opposite of my natural reaction in this case created a more positive environment for everyone.

Try a Little Chutzpa

"Courage is the price that life exacts for granting peace."
                                                — *Amelia Earhart*

In graduate school Jill Griffin learned a useful lesson out of the classroom: a little chutzpa doesn't hurt. Jill's father died when she was 13, and her mother had managed to fund her undergraduate education. Jill knew that she would have to pay for her graduate school herself.

Jill always believed that if you got good grades you could just sit back and recognition would come to you. Life taught her otherwise. She applied for an internship in the graduate business office to help finance her graduate school. Jill had a sorority sister who was not a business major. She had lower grades than Jill, and she had less financial need. However, someone had put in a good word for her, and that

~ ~

endorsement turned the tide in her favor. Her sorority sister got the internship. Jill says, "That's when I realized that it takes more than good grades to accomplish your goals."

Deciding that the time for sitting back was over, Jill camped out in front of the dean's office. When he finally agreed to see her she put her transcript in front of him. "Look at my grades," she said. "I want you to explain why I didn't get the internship." The dean looked. He saw outstanding grades. "Okay," he said. "I'll give you an assistantship for the fall semester only. It will depend on your grades what happens after that." Jill, relieved and overjoyed, knew she could make that work.

By the time she got back to the beach where she was working for the summer, Jill's chutzpa paid off with an extra bonus. She received a letter saying she had been awarded a $3,000 graduate fellowship based on her academic performance. She was sure that her visit to the dean played a part in the decision to award her the fellowship.

Telling the Truth

"I use only one set method in my little gags and that is to try and keep to the truth."
— Will Rogers

While we all agree that telling the truth is preferable to telling lies, life is not so simple as that. We want to fit in so we let things slide. There are frequently unpleasant consequences for telling the truth.

Many female U.S. Navy officers did not tell the truth about their treatment by male Navy officers. They did not speak out when they were harassed. Although, she chose a very difficult path, Lieutenant Paula Coughlin helped improve the lot for all women when she went public with the story of her mistreatment at the Tailhook Convention in Las Vegas. She had complained to the top Navy brass about sexual harassment, but her complaints were ignored.

When her story hit the public, Congressional hearings ensued leading to the resignation of the Secretary of the Navy, reassignment of six senior officials, and a Pentagon investigation. An interesting note is that the incident reported by Lieutenant Coughlin was not the first time that women had been harassed by their team mates. Yet, it was the first time that someone took the risk to report it.

Lieutenant Coughlin personally experienced a lot of anguish and pain over her decision to go public with her story. But because of her bravery and courage, the environment for women is dramatically improved in all of the armed services.

I once conducted a seminar for a group of female narcotics officers. Many of them told about sexual harassment and abuse from male officers, even chiefs who had exposed themselves to the women, urinated into their hats, pointed guns at their heads. These were tough women. They could apprehend drug criminals and face the tough existence of undercover work. These tough women, who ate nails for breakfast, broke down in tears as they told their stories. They hated signs of weakness and displays of emotion, and yet telling about their long-endured stress and indignity broke their code of silence and revealed their grief. When the "good guys" treated them as the enemy they were up against the wall and didn't know what to do. It wasn't until they told their truths that remedies could be designed to prevent the wrong doing.

The result of the conference was to design a plan to sensitize the male officers and make it clear that the unwelcome behavior would not be allowed. Steps were taken to make sure that all the officers were treated with the respect and dignity due them.

It isn't easy for us to tell the truth, and most often we are not thrown roses when we do. Ann Humphries, owner of Eticon Etiquette Consultants for Business and a frequent speaker, visited a Rotary Club. During a section of the meeting entitled "Health and Happiness," a high-level state official told an off-color joke about golfers who were promised by a genie that their wishes for themselves would be visited on their wives tenfold. The punch line was a golfer wishing for a slight heart attack so that his wife would experience a massive one and die. Doesn't it make you wish you had a term like female bashing to describe this?

Ann was offended and so told her female host who agreed with Ann's complaint. "They know better," she said. The president of the club was also a woman who admitted she had not been successful in stopping the off-color jokes.

Later Ann spoke to another local Rotary Club on the topic of gender issues. "As soon as I said gender," Ann said," the men shifted in their seats, interrupted, shouted, heckled...." The presiding officer allowed the heckling to continue and when Ann told the genie joke in reverse no one laughed. After her speech, men rushed up to tell her that they were victims of harassment, too, that they were brought up to treat ladies as ladies (despite Ann's treatment), that they put women on pedestals, and that women bit their heads off when men held a door open for them.

Ann was hurt and angered. She sent a letter protesting her treatment to the president of the club, and was sent an apology.

Not long after, a prominent attorney resigned because she was tired of the male-dominated atmosphere in her Rotary Club. The local media picked up the story and ran it, including the story about Ann's treatment at the other Rotary Club. Ann got many calls after the story was aired. Some were supportive, although many were critical. She was told, "The jokes weren't that bad," and "You are overly sensitive." She worried that her professional association would censure her for outspokenness. She felt shunned and her feeling of aloneness overpowered her feelings of support. A male friend told her to forget her objections. He said she was the only one who lost. He was wrong. Ann won for herself, and for future generations.

The Rotary Clubs discussed the matter after the press coverage and became defensive. But they could never be the same again. With extensive media attention, the "Old Boy" attitude had to change or members would face further embarrassment for the clubs.

Telling the truth was not fun and games for Ann. She was pressured from all sides to ignore her own perceptions. She felt the cold shoulder of ostracism. Doubt and fear often crowded out her thoughts of justifiable rage. But she had told the truth and caused positive change for which we owe her and other women like her a vote of thanks. When we visit a Rotary Club now we are much less likely to face those sexist jokes.

Speak Out

"The job of a good citizen is to keep [her] mouth open."

— *Gunther Grass*

When women do not speak up, telling their truths, the wrongs continue. If companies do not ensure that all employees are treated fairly power is abused. As women we need to speak up. As members of organizations we need to ensure that such behavior is not condoned. Even ignoring the behavior makes the situation worse.

Helen Gurly Brown, 72, says "I don't want to sound unsympathetic, hard, cold or tough, but in my working-girl days you always had passes by men. What's the big whoop-de-do? It's part of being an attractive woman."[56] Sorry, Helen, but you sound unsympathetic, hard, cold and tough. Men do not like being treated as sex objects and women do not like being treated as sex objects. Harassment (otherwise known as passes) impact productivity, morale, and take a disproportionate toll on women (90% of all sexual harassment suits are filed by women). It is not a part of being an attractive woman. It is part of being a second-class citizen.

There are many easy ways to speak out. Talk about challenges that you are facing with other women and with men. Such discussions can lead to developing solutions to problems and help you to clarify your own beliefs. Through discussion appropriate actions can be determined.

One situation where I spoke up was at a chamber of commerce board of directors meeting. The suggestion was made that the cheerleaders for the local football team should be invited to entertain at the membership drive kickoff meeting. I argued vehemently against the idea saying that women were the backbone of our volunteer base and that we couldn't afford to offend them. I pointed out that women were trying very hard to overcome negative stereotypes and that presenting them to our membership as sex objects was another example of reinforcing those stereotypes.

~ ~

One director asked, "What's wrong with sexuality?" He could not understand the point that sex roles and sexuality are two different subjects. And he never understood that an organization which professed to build businesses had no business promoting sexuality. (Last I heard businesses of that type were illegal.)

Two years later, this chamber of commerce was raked through the media when a mixer was planned at a restaurant named after a euphemism for women's breasts and featured waitresses in skimpy costumes. For some reason, no one was aware enough before the event to realize that a mixer at this location would be inappropriate and bring lots of bad press to the organization.

Not speaking out leads to continuation of the problems. The persecution of Navy women a la Tailhook existed for many years before Lieutenant Coughlin blew the whistle. Many times sexual harassers and women beaters have behaved in negative ways for years before a particular incident brought it to an end. Clarence Thomas may have never made it to the Supreme Court if Anita Hill had come forward earlier.

In spite of Michael Crichton's novel, *Disclosure,* in which a woman sexually harasses a man, women still bear the brunt of sexual harassment in the workplace. We cannot allow this situation to continue. Sexual harassment is not about sex, it is about power. In a "Life is Contest" pattern of relationships, women are put in their place by sexual harassment. This form of intimidation shows women that they are merely sexual objects, that their promotions can be bought by giving sexual favors and that they should be afraid of the actions of the men above them in the corporate hierarchy.

In 1990, sexual harassment complaints in the U.S. numbered 5694; the year following the Clarence Thomas hearings, complaints numbered 11,429. In 1992, 81% of Fortune 500 companies had sexual-harassment awareness programs.

After a lawsuit was filed against Del Labs, a cosmetic manufacturing company, women reported that the president of the company had sexually harassed them with some incidents dating back 30 years. Three decades ago, the term "sexual harassment" did not exist. According to a researcher at Merriam Webster, the term surfaced in 1975. In addition, in the sixties there was no recourse for sexual harassment. One woman, Susan, who considers herself the first of the many women at Del Labs the president abused, said, "You either shut your mouth or left your job."[57] Incredible turnover resulted from the abuse of female employees. Now fifteen women are suing. They are taking the risk to speak out for positive change.

The most effective response to sexual harassment is to tell the harasser emphatically to quit and that you don't like it. Speaking out is important and in any kind of abuse, vocalizing and the sooner the better is the best action. Often what happens is that the harasser (or batterer) starts with small, seemingly innocuous passes and women often make excuses for him. Inappropriate actions are much easier to stop when they are small — and any mistreatment should be vigorously addressed when it first appears. Reporting the harassment is important and speaking out against it reduces mistreatment generally.

Women, trained to defer to others, also often take blame for harassment on themselves. They may say, "I must have done something to have invited the abuse." Battered women often blame themselves for the abuse of their husbands. Harassed women often believe that they did something to engender the harassment. In a situation where there is abuse or harassment the issue of indirect blame should never be allowed. Whether or not a woman "asked for it," violence against her is wrong and against the law. Civilized human beings are not allowed to take out their aggressions on other human beings.

Pave the Way for Those That Follow

"A women's organization was the catalyst to trigger a flip-flop in my mind that I wasn't a follower, I was a leader. And in spite of my first reaction, that of fear, and a feeling I couldn't do it, I took the risk. Don't listen to other people's negativity; they filter through their own experiences. Learn to trust your own feelings. If you feel in your gut you have a winner, you have to do it no matter what."

— *Ginger Purdy*

Often we discourage ourselves from taking action because we say, "Oh well, it won't make any difference." That is an excuse we make to protect ourselves from the fear of taking action. It certainly won't make any difference if we don't try.

We don't have to make sure the situation is resolved to our satisfaction. We do have to try. All change has resulted because someone was brave enough to stand up for what she or he believed. You can't control the results, but you can make sure that when you see an injustice in the world you take the necessary steps to correct or change it.

The risks we take benefit ourselves and they benefit others who follow. Anna Quindlen, in her book *Thinking Out Loud,* tells the story of how she got her job at the *New York Times* because she was a woman. In 1978, six women

~ ~

sued the *Times* because there were so few women employed there. Quindlen was thankful for the courageousness of those women who paved the way for her to get her job at the newspaper. She is a good example of how the actions of others can pave the way for the women who are coming behind them.

The alternative to protest is continuation of the status quo. I used to belong to a toastmaster club. Off-color, wife-hating, racist, and sexist jokes were common. Chauvinism was the order of the day.

On one occasion, a female member gave a hilarious extemporaneous speech on how to improve the world. She suggested creating a pill that would sustain the feeling of euphoria that lovers experience in the early stages of relationships.

Her evaluator was a small town Baptist minister who described her as a decorator (she was an interior designer) who "decorated every room" in which she appeared. He also said that women stay with their husbands only for their checkbooks.

I was the person who rang the bell whenever a speaker said "ah" or "um" while talking. When it came time for me to report, I stood up and said, "There were no ahs today, so I decided that I would give the male chauvinist pig of the day award. It goes to Mr. X." Everyone laughed. I hope they got the message.

Later, Mr. X. came up to me and asked what he had said that was chauvinistic. I was floored. I could not believe that he could be so unaware.

Later, after I had spent hours at meetings attempting to raise consciousness on gender issues, Mr. X. sent me a note. He said, "Aren't you getting to be a Johnny One Note?"

In my final comment to the club that day, I said "Mr.

~ ~

X. had the temerity to suggest that I was getting to be a Johnny One Note. I most certainly am not a Johnny One Note. ... A Jenny One Note perhaps." The club roared.

Understand Change

"Never doubt that a small group of committed citizens can change the world; indeed it's the only thing that ever has."

— *Margaret Mead*

Part of risk is understanding and accepting change. I once heard someone say, "Nobody likes change except a wet baby." People resist change. The changing roles for men and women have brought a lot of grief to both genders. It is amusing to contemplate that many complaints about change center not so much on women taking privileges away from men, but what will happen if the playing field is level.

The complaints I hear most frequently from men, to which I've referred earlier, are the most superficial. "Women hit me over the head if I try to open the door for them."

Unhappily, all kinds of people, men, women, boys, girls, can be rude. I have opened doors for males with their arms full of bundles, and been rebuffed. Perhaps we should change the courtesy so that the first person to approach a door should be the one who holds it open for the folks who follow. This would make a lot of sense, be more civil and would grease the wheels of social intercourse without respect to gender.

Organizational Change

Women cannot make all the necessary social changes alone. The business organizations we work for must change also. Because of the history of undervaluing women's skills and contributions, businesses should embrace advancement programs designed to help women reach the top. Many present-day organizations are blind to the contributions of women. They often see what they want to see. The problem is that many of those in decision-making positions are afraid of the shift in power that may result from changing the status quo, and promoting women.

One research study showed that we tend to evaluate people based on gender rather than on ability. Two groups of people were given identical research papers, one with a female name in the byline and the other with a male name. The two groups were asked to evaluate the papers. In both groups, the paper with the male byline was rated higher.

It is difficult to deal with subconscious discrimination of this type. Good advancement programs create objective criteria which bypass unconscious gender bias.

Corporations need to institute recruitment programs which advise women of job openings and should give them opportunities to take advantage of career tracks that lead to the top. Companies which recruit women equally will benefit by the richness of talent and training available in female employees.

Sensitivity training can create awareness in the business community of unconscious bias. It can teach us how to avoid gender-biased assumptions and show us how to improve cross-gender communication skills.

~ ~

Changing Roles Bring Benefits

Women make a difference, and employers find bottom-line benefits, when women enter professions formerly closed to them, such as the construction trades. In one case, a female heavy-equipment operator consistently used less fuel per hour to run her machinery than the male operators. Her boss assumed that her equipment was the reason. However, when he put her on another piece of equipment, she also operated that equipment at $4.00 less fuel per hour. The boss discovered that the fuel economy resulted from the woman's strict adherence to the specification in the maintenance manual and careful hand-eye coordination.

Men bring benefits to the changing roles as well. A friend told me about her husband discovering a new laundry product. He broke out in a rash which the doctor diagnosed as coming from the flimsy dryer softener sheets inserted with the laundry to be dried. The doctor approved of a liquid fabric softener as a substitute. My friend explained to her husband that the liquid was introduced into the rinse cycle of the washing machine, but it was easy to miss the appropriate time to pour the liquid.

My friend's husband thought that the process was clumsy and he called the fabric softener manufacturer. He was told that the company was testing a mechanical device that dumped the fabric softener into the wash at the appropriate time automatically, eliminating the necessity for returning to the wash load.

In the first case, the female heavy-equipment operator brought benefits to the workplace by bringing fresh perspectives. In the second case, the husband brought a fresh perspective to a longstanding problem and discovered that a solution was in the works.

Changing roles bring other new perspectives. For instance, why do we not (in business) provide for the care of the children? If women stay at home to keep the children, their husband's work is actually subsidized by their unpaid work. It just makes sounder economics to consider employers as being responsible to provide for the children of employees. By doing so, companies would derive happier, more productive employees.

Be Careful of Statistics

The media continues to report with a biased eye. Studies are used to prove that women are battering men as much as men are battering women. The research that "proves" this asked women if they ever used physical violence against their husbands (such as hitting, pushing, or slapping). The researcher who conducted the studies, Richard Gelles, said, "In the majority of these cases, the women act in response to physical or psychological provocations or threats. Most use violence as a defensive reaction to violence."[59] O.J. Simpson, who is on record for beating his wife, called himself "a battered husband." Headlines blare that sexual harassment of men has doubled. In the fine print we read that the percentage has gone from 5% to 10% — and many of the cases of men being harassed are actually men being harassed by men.

Embrace Conflict

"If you have no enemies, you have not done anything important."

— Zsuzanna Emese Budapest's
mother

~ ~

When you begin to pursue your goals, one thing is certain to happen. You will experience conflict. It may be the reason we so often avoid setting goals in the first place. We act as if conflict is something to be avoided at all costs. Not avoiding conflict can give us powerful opportunities.

To tap the power of the opportunity that conflict offers, you need to realize that conflict is a gift. You should understand its sources, and how to develop techniques for embracing it.

Conflict is a Gift

"I have always grown from my problems and challenges, from the things that don't work out, that's when I've really learned."
— *Carol Burnett*

I once interviewed an employee of one of my clients. Call him Bill. I had conducted a customer service survey for the company, found a lack of team work between departments, and was beginning a team-building program to address the problem.

Bill came in with both barrels blasting. He was mad because I was seven minutes late to the manager's meeting that rainy morning (there had been a wreck on the expressway), and he was indignant about the team-building program. He berated the customer service survey. I discovered that he had sent a memo to the president of the company which said: "On a scale of one to 10, I would rate the Marketwise survey a zero."

After five minutes of Bill's abuses, I knew I hated him. I had to remind myself to breathe. My first impulse was to cut him off at the knees and slam the door. Overriding the

~ ~

temptation to conduct knee surgery on Bill, I debated other approaches to settle him down.

The summer before I had attended a workshop by Thomas Crum, author of the book *The Magic of Conflict.* Crum, a black belt in the martial art of Aikido, uses Aikido as a metaphor for dealing with conflict in the real world. The Aikido practitioner defuses the attack without hurting the attacker. Crum teaches that an attack has energy that can hurt you or can be used to take your attacker to the ground. It's you who decides how to channel the energy.

Since I had been exposed to the concept of Aikido, I contemplated possibilities other than mutilating Bill. I realized that he had a great deal of energy and that he could use his energy to help or to hinder the program. I said (as enthusiastically as I could manage while trying to unclench my teeth), "I am excited that you are so dedicated to improving this company that you were willing to take the time to prepare a memo. You obviously care a great deal and your commitment to quality will help us tremendously in building the teamwork within this company. I'm counting on you to help make it happen."

If I had not seen it, I would not have believed it. Bill settled down out of his attack mode, finished the interview very helpfully and has since become a strong supporter and advocate within the company. He has even recommended my seminars to the president and called me for my advice.

Conflict Has Rewards

I learned in this experience that it is possible for conflict to pave the way for increased effectiveness in relationships. Your personal approach and your response to criticism or to an attack determines what happens next.

~ ~

My family went on an outing to a state park. When I made the trek to the restrooms, about a quarter mile away, something was stuck in my sock and was poking my ankle. It felt like it must be a huge stick with stickers on it. I tried to shake it out a couple of times with no luck. I finally stopped and picked it out of my sock. It was smaller than a pine needle, less than half an inch long and about the diameter of a pin. I am amazed that something so small could cause so much pain. I thought that burr in my sock was like the everyday annoyances in our lives which irritate us until we remove them. Sometimes conflict motivates us to remove metaphorical burrs.

Kay Baker, a successful speaker, told me a story that is a good example of embracing conflict. Her marketing director called a woman (we'll call her Mary) who treated him very coldly. Mary was working for an organization which had been a client of Kay's, but Kay's original contact, the firm's former boss, George, was gone.

Learning that Mary had treated Kay's marketing director coldly, Kay called and set an appointment to talk to her. Kay asked Mary if there had been a problem with the work Kay had done. Mary said no. Then she confessed that she had linked Kay in her mind to George, who was intensely disliked by employees. Mary and others had concluded that Kay and he were friends. Kay told Mary that she didn't know George at all; she had just been hired to do a job, which she had performed.

Kay's conversation with Mary saved the account and resulted in many more bookings. In fact, she became friends with Mary.

Embracing conflict allows us to learn new information or correct erroneous assumptions. One day I received a letter from the Dermatology Nurses Association with an

~ ~

evaluation rating for a speech I'd given in New Orleans. I was shocked by the low score they'd assigned. I was so depressed, I momentarily considered resigning from professional speaking.

I hesitated to call the evaluator to see if there had been a mistake for fear of what I would hear. My husband, Peter, offered to call for clarification. Feeling a little guilty about being so wimpy, I agreed.

To my surprise and delight, Peter discovered that the evaluator had reversed the scores — assigning the lowest instead of the highest. I had received a 1.46 which meant more than half of the attendees had given me the highest rating. I could have gone my whole life thinking that my speech was a flop.

And what would have been the effect of such negative thinking? I might have given up speaking completely. I might have changed topics. I certainly would have thought less of myself if I had not discovered the truth about my scare.

Competition

We often assume that conflict means someone is going to lose and we want to make darn sure it isn't us. Conflict frequently can be solved so that everyone wins. I was on the board of a nonprofit organization organized into councils with committees reporting to the council chairs. One council co-chair, Sue, came to me and told me that one committee chair, Jane, was running roughshod over the volunteers and the organization's staff. Sue's co-chair, Sam, wanted to send Jane a letter firing her from the position.

I agreed with Sue that a letter would create hard feelings and might cause Jane's firm to withdraw member-

~ ~

ship. It might be possible to pick a substitute committee chair without unduly distressing Jane. I suggested that we talk to Jane and perhaps convince her to resign without hard feelings.

When we met with Jane she spent 20 minutes describing her frustrations with the committee. It was a simple matter to suggest sympathetically that perhaps another person could be found to take over her responsibilities. The relief was visible on Jane's face.

"That would be great," she said. Because we converted Jane's energy of frustration into an amicable solution everyone won.

Acknowledge Conflict

We lose so much energy when we try to keep our negative emotions from surfacing. By acknowledging our negative emotions and learning from them, we can release enormous amounts of energy. When you try too hard to please someone else you are distracting yourself from acknowledging your own negative emotions.

Once when I was trying to be friends with a self-absorbed person, I spent all of my energy on the friendship trying to please her. I was careful not to ask too much and not to make waves if I wanted something different from her. I tried to be patient when she was demanding or when she failed to show up for an appointment we had set. What I unconsciously blocked out from that experience was how I really didn't like many of her behaviors. I deluded myself, convincing myself she was a great friend, that my forbearance allowed her to enjoy herself and make her own space.

When I got mad at her, I finally began to realize that I hadn't been honest and had ignored my own deep feelings to have the relationship. Unfortunately, my anger was a very painful way to end our association. If I had allowed myself to notice the conflict, perhaps we could have negotiated a more mutually pleasing and equitable relationship.

When the Going Gets Tough

Sometimes conflicts are not with another person. They may come from within ourselves, or from our expectations. When Sandy Hogan was out of the software industry for two years she became riddled with self-doubt. Though she had proved herself in successively more challenging positions, including a high level job at Aldus Corporation, she found that software companies were looking for younger people. What does she do when the going gets tough? "I feel the feelings," says Sandy. "I allow myself to do that." Then she does something creative for two or three days without feeling guilty. She calls her dearest friends and tells them about the situation. Then, armed again with her own sense of self, she begins to pursue her goals again. "In those times when I have felt like I'm unraveling, I am really re-weaving. I just can't see the pattern yet." Eventually, Sandy realized there was a greater purpose to the situation. Time creates a different perspective.

When the going gets tough, Barb Schwarz reminds herself to stay centered. "People get stuck in the problem," Barb says. "Take what action you can." Barb realized at the age of five that she couldn't control what her parents did. To affect her life, it had to come from her.

Barb's daughter, Andrea, was in an auto accident when she was 18. Andrea had been an honor student, a downhill skier and a hopeful for the Olympics. She came home from the hospital brain-damaged with the capabilities of a three-

year-old. Barb came home and said, "What can we do about
it?" Her mother had been a world class worrier and long ago
Barb had decided not to worry. Barb reaffirmed, "I am not
going to start worrying now." Barb decided to be thankful
for what she did have. She was grateful that Andrea had not
been killed. Three years ago, Andrea couldn't put a piece of
paper in an envelope. Now she helps in Barb's business. She
now has the mind capacity of a 12 to 18-year-old. "We've
had stuff happen to us," Barb says. "And yet, I believe
everything is in a perfect state. It is hard for the human mind
to comprehend the big picture. I am thankful for everything,
and I believe God is in everything."

When stuff happens, Barb advises that you stand back
and ask, "What can I do?" Don't examine the situation to
death. Try to look at the bigger picture. Our inner powers
know. We all have those powers.

Elisabeth Kubler-Ross faced conflicts as she pursued
her life's work. She has accomplished many breakthroughs
in understanding death and dying, and she has become
recognized internationally. Interestingly, she was frequently
criticized for her work. She was the first professional to ask
terminally ill patients about their experiences and report on
her findings. Her academic colleagues criticized her and
called her a vulture preying on the pain of others. The
patients, however, appreciated the opportunity to share their
burdens. Her work has given many people, both patients and
their families, hope and encouragement.

Elisabeth described the benefits of embracing conflict
when she said, "To love means never to be afraid of the
windstorms of life: Should you shield the canyons from the
windstorms, you would never see the true beauty of their
carvings. I hope people choose to expose themselves to
these windstorms so that at the end of their own days they

will be proud to look in the mirror and be pleased with the carvings of their own canyon."[58]

Techniques for Tapping Conflict

To be able to use the energy available from conflict you must first place yourself in what Aikido artists describe as the mental and physical state of being "centered." The concept of being physically centered comes from physics. Every object (animate or inanimate) has a physical center of gravity defined as the point on which the object can be balanced. The center of gravity in the human body is about two inches below the navel. When the martial artist is physically centered you cannot easily throw her off balance and she can channel the energy of the attack. If the artist is off balance the attacker can defeat her easily. This is true for us in a metaphorical sense as well.

Try this for yourself with a partner. Facing the same direction and standing side by side, place your hand nearest your partner on her chest. Have your partner think about her head. Gently push until her body moves a little bit. Notice how much pressure you must exert to begin to move her. Then have your partner focus her attention on her center (about two inches below the navel). Again, gently push your partner on the chest. Notice that it requires much more pressure to make her move, if she moves at all.

The quality of being centered in your life creates balanced emotions. Remember those times in your life when everything was balanced and in harmony? Times like these are the ones when you are physically, mentally, and spiritually centered. In these moments, conflict exerts much less influence and you can gain the benefits of the unexposed energy potential of the conflict.

~ ~

To increase your centeredness make sure you have plenty of balance in your life. How do you do that? Physically, you exercise, eat nutritious foods, get adequate rest, and adequate play. Mentally, you read, look, and listen to new ideas and expand your awareness as you travel through life. Spiritually, you meditate, worship, and spend time getting to know yourself. When these three important areas of your life are in balance, you can receive the energy potential of conflict and to use it to accomplish your goals.

Fun, quiet time, physical fitness, celebration and humor all add to your physical and mental health and prepare you for accepting the gifts that conflict brings. In a department, allow time at all staff meetings to clear the air. Allow for honest discussion of hurt feelings, misunderstandings, and the telling of uncomfortable truths. The one certain thing about uncomfortable truths is that without airing they become more uncomfortable.

To increase your ability to channel energy think of conflict in terms of a strategy. If you are developing a strategic business plan you want as much information as possible about your target market, competition, price of goods, and all other contributing factors. To resolve a conflict, you also want to have as much information as possible. Where do you get it? By asking questions and listening to the responses.

When I was first married, I got up one Saturday morning and announced, "I am going to make coffee cake!" I love coffee cake and I used to love baking. My husband, Peter, said, "Oh, no. Don't make coffee cake. I hate coffee cake." So, I didn't make coffee cake. About a month later, full of optimism that he would have forgotten that he said he didn't like coffee cake, I again got up and announced, "I am going to make coffee cake!" Again, Peter said, "Oh, no.

Don't make coffee cake. I hate coffee cake." So, again, I didn't make coffee cake. This scene was repeated often over the next three years.

After three years the honeymoon was over. I got up one Saturday morning and hands on hips, I declared, *"I'm* going to make coffee cake today. I don't *care* if you don't like coffee cake, I'm going to make coffee cake." Pausing briefly, I thought and on impulse asked, "Besides, why don't you like coffee cake?"

"Because," said Peter, "I don't like coffee."

I wanted to choke him. When I think of coffee cake, I think of a pastry with nuts, cinnamon and possibly some icing. When Peter heard coffee cake, he thought of a cake made out of coffee. When he learned my definition (of course, mine was the right definition) of coffee cake, it turned out he loved it! The resolution to this conflict was easy. I asked one question, and the conflict was solved.

Many of our conflicts are exactly that easy. We don't understand the point of view of our opponent. If we understood each other's point of view we might not be opponents at all.

Sometimes, by ourselves, we can try a different point of view and we immediately have a different impression of the conflict. For instance, rather than labeling a disagreement as a fight take the point of view that the disagreement is an opportunity to learn more about the other person.

Once after I had finished a seminar a nurse came up and told me that her husband was a dermatologist. She explained that on one occasion during the absence of his surgical nurse, he pressed his wife into service and during surgery smartly slapped a pair of scissors into her hand. Offended by his rudeness, the wife's first impulse was to walk out. "How could he do that to me?" she asked herself.

~ ~

"Here I am trying to help him and all he can do is return the favor with rudeness."

Later at home, she confronted her husband and demanded to know why he had slapped the scissors in her hand. Surprised, he told her that his action was operating room procedure. To make certain that instruments were not dropped, nurses and doctors slapped them vigorously in each other's hands. Her anger dissipated. She solved her conflict by sensibly asking her husband about the situation rather than letting it build up.

The perspective of discovery helps tremendously in tapping the power of conflict. Try something and see how it works. If it works well, it is a winner. If it doesn't work, dismiss it and move onto the next possibility. Thomas Edison used this principle in discovering the light bulb. Although it took him 10,000 tries to invent the light bulb, he viewed it as 9,999 discoveries of ways not to invent the light bulb.

In a conflict situation, ask yourself what does this look like from the other side? Ask the person how she or he came to believe what she or he believed.

Frequently emotions prevent us from looking at a conflict situation from a strategic viewpoint. We are angry, defensive, and frustrated. It is impossible to be angry and centered at the same time. Our emotional response to the conflict hinders our tapping the gifts which the conflict has to offer.

Quick Tips for Conflicts

To embrace conflict try these tips:
- If you are being verbally attacked, step outside your defensive self and the fear that informs you

that you are going to be hurt. Look at the attack in terms of strategy. What is it the other person wants, and how can you redirect her energy to helping her get what she wants?

- A situation is good or bad depending on your viewpoint. Ask yourself: Where is the energy in this situation? Where could it be applied to help my goals the most?

- We often learn the most from situations which seem the most difficult. When lifting weights, muscles are built with heavier weights. Likewise, we learn and grow most from the situations that stretch our mental, creative muscles. Ask yourself: What can I learn from this situation? What does it tell me about myself and about the others involved?

- Write yourself (or some dear friend) a letter telling all about the conflict. Give yourself a time limit, say 10 minutes, and write whatever comes into your mind without censoring it. Keep your hand moving and don't pause. Write down the different voices that come into your mind as you write. This technique helps you clarify the thoughts that are rumbling around in your head, and some new awareness results. Don't send the letter. Burn it if you like.

Chapter Nine
Diligence

~ ~

"The world is round and the place which may
seem like the end may also be only the beginning."
— Ivy Baker Priest

Evaluate your progress weekly, monthly and yearly.
Create a chart to visually follow your progress.
Redo the process every year. Goal setting is cyclical.
First, you set goals, then you make plans, then you
work the plan. Then you evaluate your progress, then you
revise your goals and plans, then you set new goals and
begin the cycle all over again.

Have Patience with the Process

"You are a part of the universe, no less than the
stars and trees, and you have a right to be here.

~ ~

And whether it is clear to you or not, no doubt the
universe is unfolding as it should."
                                    — *Desiderata*

It doesn't always seem as if you are making progress.
Once when I conducted a week-long series of town hall
meetings in South Texas, I woke up achy and sore. I thought
it was because I had been tense at the session the night
before. The session was taking longer than I wanted, the
pace was lagging and I was worried the participants would
be impatient to conclude the presentation.

Ironically, later I found that I got rave reviews for that
session. I had felt like the hare encouraging the tortoise to
go faster. What I discovered was that my urgency, my sense
of timing, didn't match the expectations of the participants.

My contact told me the city administrators had praised
the job I had done. One participant revealed that he had
written his colleague who was paying my fee, and told him
that I had done a great job, and he should write me a letter
of appreciation. The positive strokes came at a good time
and helped my confidence and state of mind. I loved it!

My inner critic immediately started saying, "Well, this
isn't that hard to do."

My defense said, "Yes, it is. I use a strategic approach
to get the groups to work well together, I stay attuned to
group dynamics and my pleasant, pleasing personality helps
things go so well."

We all need to give ourselves good feedback when we
are feeling less than confident. Argue with your internal
critic! Don't let the voice of criticism stop you from moving
forward. Progress is difficult to measure and sometimes you
can't see it. Give it time. You will measure forward advance
eventually if you keep going.

Richard Ott wrote about the "jet" effect.[60] He says that when you are flying in a jet, you are going very fast, but because you are far from the ground, it may look like you are progressing very slowly. If you are working on your goals, it may seem like you are progressing very slowly. In reality, your perspective may not show you how much progress you are making. Each step may seem small but every small step takes you closer to your objectives and to your goals. Look back at where you were six months ago to get a better perspective.

Measure Success by Your Standards

"I was raised to sense what someone wanted me to be and be that kind of person. It took me a long time not to judge myself through someone else's eyes."

— *Sally Field*

As you observe others, avoid the trap of comparing yourself to them, especially in such ways as, "Gosh, by the time Mozart was my age, he'd been dead ten years!"

A great question to ask yourself every day is, "How am I going to set up my life so I can express me?" If you are not expressing you, who will? And expressing yourself does not mean worrying about pleasing others. Expressing yourself means looking inward and setting up your life to be true to your dreams.

A better question than, "Am I measuring up?" is "Are my actions taking me closer to my dreams?"

Rather than ask, "Does anybody like/love/approve of me?" ask "What are my dreams and how can my life express me?"

If women are to succeed by our definition of success, we have to measure ourselves by our own standards.

Comparing ourselves to others is a part of the "Life is Contest" approach. It also keeps us in the Venus trap. When we compare ourselves to others, we most frequently conclude we are somehow inadequate. We often think we are wrong because we are different. Sometimes we conclude others are wrong because they are different. Either way, we are the ones who lose. We lose our self-respect and our direction. Avoid comparisons, realizing that you are on your own path. Whether you are doing better or worse than others is irrelevant to your path.

I once walked the Rio Grande hiking trail at Bentsen Rio Grande State Park. It was deserted on a Tuesday in November. I passed three people on the trail and only saw half a dozen others on the roads in the park. The cool air kissed my cheeks. Overhead soared a hawk with a wide white band on his rump, and I heard a bird with a yellow breast that sounded like a cat. I passed a stalk of grass that had a down feather hanging from it. I delighted in the decoration. It seemed even nature decorated the greenery for the pleasure of my eyes.

I passed a woman who said, "I thought I was the only one who did this," in a tone that suggested no one else would be so crazy as to hike these trails alone.

I thought about how, as women, we are separated from each other and that our separation keeps us from knowing that there are others just like us. Why should women enjoying themselves in nature be unusual? Let's measure ourselves by our own standards.

~ ~

Persistence

"When you get into a tight place and everything goes against you, 'till it seems as though you could not hang on a minute longer, never give up then, for that is the place and time that the tide will turn."
— *Harriet Beecher Stowe*

At the zoo, I read that cheetahs don't stalk their prey, they just run until they catch it. But they are only successful in 10 to 30 percent of their chases. I thought how persistent they are. We humans give up a lot of times before we get to the fourth or the tenth try. How would it be if the cheetah said, "I give up. I tried once and I can't catch that supper I was going after."

Another way to encourage yourself to persist is to remember that progress is not linear. There are times when you will not see progress at all. There are even times when you will seem to go backward. However, if you persist there will be times of progress, and sometimes rapid progress.

Here is a concept I learned from Michael Gelb's book, *The Art of Juggling.* When learning any skill (the attempt to achieve any goal is an example of skill or multiple skills) sometimes you will progress, sometimes you will plateau, and sometimes you will regress. This *always* happens. Most often, following a regression is a time of rapid progress.

If you anticipate these ups and downs, you will not be so upset during those times when progress is slow or nonexistent. If you expect your progress to be a straight line upward, then when a regression or a plateau comes along, you are more likely to quit.

If you don't quit, you will likely find immediately following the plateau is a quantum leap forward. The next

~ ~

time you have a plateau, or a regression, tell yourself you are getting ready for a leap forward. Keep on keeping on and soon you will have fulfilled your prophecy.

Take Time Out to Recharge

"If you have made mistakes ... there is always another chance for you ... you may have a fresh start any moment you choose, for this thing we call 'failure' is not the falling down, but the staying down."

— *Mary Pickford*

Be gentle with yourself as you take those difficult steps. It takes time and energy to develop the kind of excellence you desire. In the process, take time to recharge yourself by finding a special resting place that is meaningful to you. My resting place is Big Bend, Texas.

To me, the air and the land in West Texas desert country is medicinal. When I'm there, I feel healed and centered in myself. I feel happy and content.

Once, when I was at the frayed end of my rope, I went to Big Bend. I was spent, burned out after a year of 14-hour days earning my M.B.A. while caring for my small children. When I graduated, I expected a sense of relief, but I felt even more stressed than ever. I began to have nightmares in which I had major reports due at school which I hadn't even started to prepare.

Days weren't much better than those nightmares. The kids and Peter and I passed around strep throat for three months, with at least one of us sick for the whole time. Finally, the doctor started treating the whole family at once, and it took two rounds of antibiotics before we were cured.

I knew I had to get away for a while because I felt as if I were disappearing completely into the duties I had to complete. I outfitted my mini-van with plastic garbage bag curtains, sleeping bag mattress, flashlights and books to read at night. On the drive to Big Bend, I kept repeating joyfully to myself: "I can do anything *I* want to do. I can do anything I *want* to do!"

In reality, the first day I spent most of it driving because I was too scared to get out of the car. I only stopped at a picnic area for lunch, and to get gas. That day I eventually drove about 400 miles in a huge circle viewing the countryside around Big Bend.

By the second day, I had calmed down enough to decide that I would hike a trail, and so I did. I had gotten books describing the hiking trails. I chose trails I had hiked before on earlier trips to Big Bend and I tried new trails that sounded like fun.

About the fourth day I was there, I drove down the Ross Maxwell Scenic Drive. I enjoyed looking at the cacti and flowers of the desert. The flowers were spectacular because it had been an unusually wet fall resulting in a glorious spring. At one place, I saw many cholla cacti covered with yellow blooms.

Then I stopped at a trail head and began a hike across the desert. I had gone about a quarter of a mile when I saw another cholla cactus that had buds on it. I stopped and thought, this cactus will be blooming in about two weeks. As I looked at the cactus, I realized that right in front of my face, at eye level, was a tiny hummingbird sitting on a nest. I held my breath and my heart was about bursting out of my chest. I wanted to jump up and down and scream and yell. Look at this! Look at this wonderful sight! There was absolutely no one on the trail to share this with. I grabbed

~ ~

my camera and took a roll of film. I soaked up the awe and the beauty of this tiny bird, hatching her eggs in the desert air on a cactus. I knew how she felt. When I was completely filled with her beauty I walked on down the trail to the end, turned around and began my way back. I longed to share the gift with someone else.

About half the way back, I passed a man coming toward me. "Oh, did you see the hummingbird on the nest?" I asked excitedly. The man acted like I was an escaped inmate from a mental institution. I could hear him thinking, "Please don't hurt me. Go away quietly." I walked on my way and he walked his way (the other direction from the hummingbird.) I passed the hummingbird again. She was still sitting. I took several more pictures.

Reluctantly, I bid her farewell and walked back toward my van. As I neared the parking area, two men were walking toward me. Their arms were full of huge scopes — looked to me like telescopes. "Oh, don't miss the humming-bird sitting on the nest on a cholla cactus." I explained to them exactly where she was. They listened patiently, and we talked for a minute. "Now, where exactly was she?" they asked at the end of our conversation.

"Oh, come on. I'll show you." So we tromped on down the trail to the hummingbird. "Ah, yes," said one of the men. "That is a Lucifer's hummingbird." "How do you know that?" I asked. The man whipped out a bird book from his waist pack and flipped to the pages where there were a dozen hummingbirds. They looked pretty much the same to me. All light green and about the same size. "See how she has a black line behind her eye and how her bill curves? Only the Lucifer's hummingbird looks like that."

The men told me that they had come to that trail that day because they were looking for the Lucifer's hummingbird, which can only be found in the deserts of Texas and in Mexico. It is named Lucifer's because it lives in the blazing heat of the desert. I had shown them the way to their goal and had gotten a huge gift myself.

Because I had ventured out on my own, I was given a gift that otherwise I may never have been given. I didn't set out to find the Lucifer's hummingbird, and I didn't set out to help other people achieve their goal. Even so, both of those gifts were given to me just because I took the risk. By setting my actions in motion gifts that I never expected came to me. I also achieved the goal that I intended, I returned to my life with renewed energy, commitment, and the zest to continue afresh.

Similar gifts will come to you as you follow your dream. You will help others, and you will find gifts in your life. You will give and you will receive. Struggles will give you the gift of emerging stronger by riding through the storms. Love your dream, discover ways to proceed, design your life accordingly. All of your experiences have helped make you who you are and will help you as you continue to pursue your dream.

"Aim at a high mark and you'll hit it. No, not the first time, nor the second time. Maybe not the third. But keep on aiming and keep on shooting for only practice will make you perfect. Finally you'll hit the bull's-eye of success."

— Annie Oakley

Chapter Ten
Beyond Dragontalk

~ ~

Once upon a time, in a village called Yore, a baby girl
was born and her parents named her Diryl. At Diryl's birth,
when she first opened her mouth, instead of the usual cry, a
song burst forth. Now Yorians were afraid of girls that sang
and her parents taught her early not to sing but to talk. As a
matter of fact, Diryl forgot that she was born with a song in
her mouth. She heard some of the boys in the village sing
many different wonderful songs, and her heart sometimes
felt heavy when she heard singing, although she couldn't
remember why.

By the time Diryl grew into a young woman the village
was often attacked by a dragon who lived in a cavern
beyond the woods. The dragon burned down homes and
killed many villagers. The villagers fought the dragon with
all their might, trying to kill it and save the village, but none
succeeded and all those who tried were killed. The villagers

~ ~

lived in constant danger, but they learned to hide whenever there was firestone on the wind.

One day, Diryl discovered that she was shrinking. At first she thought she was imagining it, but sure enough, she marked her height on the doorway of her hut, and the next day the top of her head didn't quite reach the mark. Day after day, her marks were lower and lower. Diryl worried that she might actually disappear. Surprisingly, none of the villagers noticed her problem but still Diryl was afraid and ashamed. Then one night a fairy came to Diryl in a dream and told her that she was shrinking because she had abandoned her birth gift of singing. Diryl woke with a start, and she was more afraid than before. Women were not allowed to sing and the villagers would punish her if she sang. Still, a tiny part of her heart felt lighter than it had since she was a babe.

Diryl decided that if she went into the woods to sing the villagers would never know. So, she went into the middle of the woods and she sang. Her voice was a bit croaky at first, but after a few times she remembered her songs and her voice learned to carry the notes into the wind. At first, Diryl sang very quietly in fear that the villagers would hear. But soon, her songs gained strength and power and she could no longer sing quietly. She went further and further into the woods to hide her songs.

One day, however, Diryl grew tired of singing alone in the woods. "There's no reason I shouldn't sing in the village," she said to herself and so she returned home singing her song. The villagers heard her sing and dragged Diryl to a village council meeting. They tied her hands and legs. Diryl tried to explain about how she had been shrinking, but they did not believe her. Any woman who disobeyed the village order had to be banished. Diryl argued, and then got angry. Who decided women shouldn't sing anyway? Her arguments fell on deaf ears, but Diryl could not escape. The villagers threw her into the dragon's cavern. She fell to the floor and found herself all alone.

Her heart pounding, Diryl began to cry. She knew the dragons were not far away and that she would die soon. She cried and cried and soon, there was a lake of tears surrounding her on the floor. The tears began to run into the dark recess of the cavern, where the dragon was sleeping. Awakened, the dragon came to see what was creating the flood in the cave.

There was Diryl crying. The dragon opened its mouth to breathe fire, but the tears had wet its throat and so the fire was extinguished. The dragon told Diryl it would eat her when its fire returned, but in the meantime she must tidy the cave, wash the dishes, and grind firestone for its supper. Then the dragon curled up and fell back to sleep.

At first, Diryl tried to escape, but the mouth of the cavern was high above her. She knew that even if she did what the dragon ordered she would die. Exhausted from her escape attempts, Diryl lay down to rest. She thought and thought what to do. She knew that she wanted to live and that she wanted somehow to return to her village. She didn't think tidying the cave or grinding the firestone would help.

She decided to try killing the dragon before it awoke. She found a sword laying on the floor of the cave beyond the sleeping dragon. She grabbed the sword, and then holding the sword high above her head she plunged it into the dragons neck. Instead of dying, the dragon split into three. Diryl was surrounded now by the fire of three dragons. She was so frightened that she couldn't breathe. "If there were just one dragon," Diryl thought, "then I could manage. But with three dragons, it is just too much. They

~ ~

are going to kill me." Even though the fire was loud, under-
neath the sound of the fire, Diryl could hear the dragons
muttering. With the noise of the fire of all of the dragons she
couldn't make out the words.

"Since I am going to die anyway perhaps if I go closer
I can at least hear what the dragons are saying." So,
gathering all her courage, Diryl approached the dragons.
Sure enough, she could make out the words. The dragons
were saying, "You must do all the tasks. You're not good
enough. No one will ever love you." The fire from their
breath burned her body and singed her hair.

Knowing she would die, Diryl tried to comfort herself.
She began to sing her songs. The dragons were very
surprised, and they merged back into one. The dragon
forgot all about eating Diryl and began to cry even as it
breathed fire. Diryl was moved by the sorrow of the dragon
and setting her fear aside, she went up to the dragon and
kissed it on the cheek. The fiery breath faded and the dragon
said, "Sing, Diryl, sing. Nobody can sing like you do." Then
the dragon said, "Diryl, you must bring your song back to
the village. I will help you return."

The dragon beat its wings and gently lifted Diryl up
and out of the cave. Together they returned to the village,
and together they sang with all their might. The villagers
heard the sound and came to see what was happening. When
they saw Diryl and the dragons, they drew back in fear. But
the song entered their hearts and minds, and soon the
villagers joined hands and danced in a circle around Diryl
and the dragons. Forever after, the dragon lived in peace
with the village and the village benefitted from the beauty
of Diryl's songs.

And so, I ask you: "Are you singing the song you came to sing?"

Footnotes

~ ~

Chapter One

1. Johnson, Lindsey and Joyner-Kersee, Jackie. *A Woman's Place ... Is Everywhere.* Master Media, New York, N.Y., 1994, page 106.

2. Johnson, Lindsey and Joyner-Kersee, Jackie. *A Woman's Place ... Is Everywhere.* Master Media, New York, N.Y., 1994, page 105.

3. Johnson, Lindsey and Joyner-Kersee, Jackie. *A Woman's Place ... Is Everywhere.* Master Media, New York, N.Y., 1994, page 111.

4. *Wall Street Journal,* New York, N. Y., October 18, 1994, page B11.

5. Johnson, Lindsey and Joyner-Kersee, Jackie. *A Woman's Place ... Is Everywhere.* Master Media, New York, N.Y., 1994, page 197.

6. Hobday, Jose, O.S.F., "Neither Late Nor Working," *Creation Spirituality,* May/June 1992, page 20.

Chapter Two

7. Forbes, Malcolm. *Women Who Made A Difference.* Simon and Schuster, New York, N.Y., 1990, page 21.

8. Forbes, Malcolm. *Women Who Made A Difference.* Simon and Schuster, New York, N.Y., 1990, page 31.

9. Forbes, Malcolm. *Women Who Made A Difference.* Simon and Schuster, New York, N.Y., 1990, page 17.

10. Forbes, Malcolm. *Women Who Made A Difference.* Simon and Schuster, New York, N.Y., 1990, page 37-38.

11. Forbes, Malcolm. *Women Who Made A Difference.* Simon and Schuster, New York, N.Y., 1990, page 63.

12. Johnson, Lindsey and Joyner-Kersee, Jackie. A *Woman's Place ... Is Everywhere.* Master Media, New York, N.Y., 1994, page 195.

~ ~

13. Cantor, Dorothy W. and Bernay, Toni with Stoess, Jean. *Women in Power.* Houghton Mifflin, Boston, New York, London, 1992, page 161.

14. Cantor, Dorothy W. and Bernay, Toni with Stoess, Jean. *Women in Power.* Houghton Mifflin, Boston, New York, London, 1992, page 164.

15. Johnson, Lindsey and Joyner-Kersee, Jackie. *A Woman's Place ... Is Everywhere.* Master Media, New York, N.Y., 1994, page 200.

16. Johnson, Lindsey and Joyner-Kersee, Jackie. *A Woman's Place ... Is Everywhere.* Master Media, New York, N.Y., 1994, page 201.

17. Cantor, Dorothy W. and Bernay, Toni with Stoess, Jean. *Women in Power.* Houghton Mifflin, Boston, New York, London, 1992, page 160.

18. Cantor, Dorothy W. and Bernay, Toni with Stoess, Jean. *Women in Power.* Houghton Mifflin, Boston, New York, London, 1992, page 142.

19. Johnson, Lindsey and Joyner-Kersee, Jackie. *A Woman's Place ... Is Everywhere.* Master Media, New York, N.Y., 1994, page 86.

20. LaTeef, Nelda. *Working Women for the 21st Century.* Williamson Publishing, Charlotte, Vermont, 1992, page 8.

~ ~

21. Johnson, Lindsey and Joyner-Kersee, Jackie. *A Woman's Place ... Is Everywhere.* Master Media, New York, N.Y., 1994, page 86.

22. LaTeef, Nelda. *Working Women for the 21st Century.* Williamson Publishing, Charlotte, Vermont, 1992, page 7.

23. Johnson, Lindsey and Joyner-Kersee, Jackie. *A Woman's Place ... Is Everywhere.* Master Media, New York, N.Y., 1994, page 80.

24. LaTeef, Nelda. *Working Women for the 21st Century.* Williamson Publishing, Charlotte, Vermont, 1992, page 9.

25. LaTeef, Nelda. Working *Women for the 21st Century.* Williamson Publishing, Charlotte, Vermont, 1992, page 9.

26. Johnson, Lindsey and Joyner-Kersee, Jackie. *A Woman's Place ... Is Everywhere.* Master Media, New York, N.Y., 1994, page 86.

27. Johnson, Lindsey and Joyner-Kersee, Jackie. *A Woman's Place ... Is Everywhere.* Master Media, New York, N.Y., 1994, page 75.

28. Johnson, Lindsey and Joyner-Kersee, Jackie. *A Woman's Place ... Is Everywhere.* Master Media, New York, N.Y., 1994, page 78.

29. Federally registered trademark of Barb Schwarz.

30. Federally registered trademark of Barb Schwarz.

Chapter Three

31. Scannell, Edward E. and Newstron, John W. *More Games Trainers Play.* McGraw Hill, Inc., New York,N.Y., 1983, page 237.

Chapter Four

32. Goldberg, Natalie, *Writing Down The Bones.* Shambhalla, Boston, Ma., 1986, page 38.

33. Aronson, David. "The Inside Story," *Teaching Tolerance.* Spring 1995, page 26.

34. Eisler, Riane. *The Chalice And The Blade,* Harper-Collins, Inc., New York, N.Y., 1987, page 28.

35. Cantor, Dorothy W. and Bernay, Toni with Stoess, Jean. *Women in Power.* Houghton Mifflin, Boston, New York, London, 1992, page 71.

36. *Wall Street Journal,* New Yorl, N.Y., September 19, 1994.

37. Raben, Gail. Forthcoming book.

Chapter Five

38. Agonito, Rosemary, Ph.D. *No More "Nice Girl."* Bob Adams, Inc. Massachusetts, 1993.

39. King, Laurel. *Women of Power.* Celestial Arts Berkeley, California, 1989, page 137.

40. King, Laurel. *Women of Power.* Celestial Arts Berkeley, California, 1989, page 229.

41. Feinberg, Mortimer R. *Effective Psychology for Managers.*

42. King, Laurel. *Women of Power.* Celestial Arts Berkeley, California, 1989, page 111.

Chapter Six

43. Johnson, Lindsey and Joyner-Kersee, Jackie. *A Woman's Place ... Is Everywhere.* Master Media, New York, N.Y., 1994, page 105.

44. Eisler, Riane. *The Chalice And The Blade,* Harper-Collins, Inc., New York, N.Y., 1987, page xviii.

45. Lerner, Harriet Goldhor, Ph.D. *The Dance of Anger.* Harper and Row, New York, N.Y., 1985, page 22.

46. Lerner, Harriet Goldhor, Ph.D. *The Dance of Anger.* Harper and Row, New York, N.Y., 1985, page 22.

47. Lerner, Harriet Goldhor, Ph.D. *The Dance of Anger.* Harper and Row, New York, N.Y., 1985, page 21.

48. Aronson, David. "Heroic Possibilities (Interview with Michael Dorris)." *Teaching Tolerance.* Spring 1995, page 15.

49. Lerner, Harriet Goldhor, Ph.D. *The Dance of Anger.* Harper and Row, New York, N.Y., 1985, page 1.

50. Lerner, Harriet Goldhor, Ph.D. *The Dance of Anger.* Harper and Row, New York, N.Y., 1985, page 2.

51. Kolbenschlag. *Kiss Sleeping Beauty Good-bye.* Bantam Books, New York, N.Y., page 76.

52. Phil Donahue, March 23, 1995.

Chapter Seven

53. Kanter, Rosabeth Moss. "Power failure in management circuits." *Harvard Business Review,* July-August 1979, page 65.

54. Kanter, Rosabeth Moss. "Power failure in management circuits." *Harvard Business Review,* July-August 1979, page 67.

55. Kanter, Rosabeth Moss. "Power failure in management circuits." *Harvard Business Review,* July-August 1979, page 66-67.

Chapter Eight

56. *Newsweek,* September 12, 1994, page 50.

57. *Newsweek,* September 12, 1994, page 49.

58. Kubler-Ross, Elisabeth and Marshaw, Mal. *To Live Until We Say Good-Bye.* Prentice Hall, Englewood Cliffs, New Jersey, 1978, page 155.

59- EXTRA! *Update,* October 1994, page 1.

Chapter Nine

60. Ott, Richard. *Unleashing Productivity,* Irwin Professional Publishing, New York, N.Y., 1994, pages 131-134.

For More Information ...

As a consultant, speaker, and trainer, Robin Bowman successfully develops dynamic, custom-tailored programs that increase productivity and improve bottom line performance. Robin helps organizations tap the potential of their employees by improving teamwork.

Robin, a member of the National Speakers Association, frequently presents:
- keynote speeches
- seminars
- workshops
- strategic planning retreats
  on such topics as:
- Escaping the Venus Trap
- Team building
- Gender issues
- Communication

For more information and to schedule her for your organization, please call:

800-864-5390

or

210-545-5881

To order additional copies of

Escaping The Venus Trap

Please send _____ copies at $14.95 for each book, plus $3.50 shipping and handling for each book.

Enclosed is my check or money order of $_____
or [ ] Visa   [ ] MasterCard
#_____ Exp. Date ____/____
Signature _____

Name _____
Street Address _____
City _____
State _____ Zip _____
Phone _____

(Advise if recipient and shipping address are different from above.)

For credit card orders call:
1-800-895-7323

or
Return this order form to:

BookPartners
P.O. Box 922
Wilsonville, OR 97070